ASHE Higher Education Report: Volume 36, Number 5
Kelly Ward, Lisa E. Wolf-Wendel, Series Editors

Non-Tenure-Track Faculty in Higher Education: Theories and Tensions

Adrianna Kezar

Cecile Sam

D1444903

Non-Tenure-Track Faculty in Higher Education: Theories and Tensions
Adrianna Kezar and Cecile Sam
ASHE Higher Education Report: Volume 36, Number 5
Kelly Ward, Lisa E. Wolf-Wendel, Series Editors

ISSN 1551-6970   electronic ISSN 1554-6306   ISBN 978-1-1180-1405-9

The ASHE Higher Education Report is part of the Jossey-Bass Higher and Adult
Education Series and is published six times a year by Wiley Subscription Services,
Inc., A Wiley Company, at Jossey-Bass, 989 Market Street, San Francisco,
California 94103-1741.

For subscription information, see the Back Issue/Subscription Order Form
in the back of this volume.

CALL FOR PROPOSALS: Prospective authors are strongly encouraged to contact
Kelly Ward (kaward@wsu.edu) or Lisa Wolf-Wendel (lwolf@ku.edu). See "About
the ASHE Higher Education Report Series" in the back of this volume.

Visit the Jossey-Bass Web site at **www.josseybass.com.**

Printed in the United States of America on acid-free recycled paper.

The ASHE Higher Education Report is indexed in CIJE: Current Index to Jour-
nals in Education (ERIC), Current Abstracts (EBSCO), Education Index/Abstracts
(H.W. Wilson), ERIC Database (Education Resources Information Center),
Higher Education Abstracts (Claremont Graduate University), IBR & IBZ: Inter-
national Bibliographies of Periodical Literature (K.G. Saur), and Resources in
Education (ERIC).

Advisory Board

The ASHE Higher Education Report Series is sponsored by the Association for the Study of Higher Education (ASHE), which provides an editorial advisory board of ASHE members.

Contents

Executive Summary

The American faculty is changing. Tenure-track appointments that were once the majority employment type are no longer the established norm of higher education; approximately 65 percent of all new faculty appointments are now nontenure track. Part-time non-tenure-track faculty appointments now make up the bulk of that percentage. Despite these changes, many higher education institutions still operate as though non-tenure-track faculty are a supplementary workforce, while the percentage of non-tenure-track faculty continues to grow.

With the growing majority of non-tenure-track faculty, questions arise. Who are these faculty? What are their experiences? What does this faculty mean for undergraduate instruction and students? What is the role of tenure in higher education? How did higher education attain this majority of non-tenure-track faculty? Where does higher education go from here?

This monograph synthesizes and critiques the theoretical underpinnings used to understand non-tenure-track faculty. The authors analyze the dominant theories from four disciplines—economic, sociological, psychological and social-psychological, and organizational—and explore their applicability as well as limitations. These theoretical foundations from many studies often have their own set of assumptions made about non-tenure-track faculty such as determining their status as laborers or professionals, and these assumptions shape interpretations of the data. The authors argue that the topic of non-tenure-track faculty has been understudied and that theories applied are narrow in scope. They encourage the use of more interdisciplinary theories and the use of multiple theories or disciplines simultaneously in studies.

One of the goals of this monograph is to advance the current dialogue about the role of non-tenure-track faculty in higher education and the next steps toward the future of this faculty. The authors compare empirical data with the preconceived notions, ideologies, and anecdotal evidence to challenge stereotypes and misconceptions that people may have of non-tenure-track faculty, their quality, and their experience.

Some of the major themes and recommendations that form the foundation on which this monograph is based are as follows:

Non-tenure-track faculty are a heterogeneous mixture of people who differ greatly in terms of employment, experiences, job descriptions, and motivations. Reliable institutional, state, and national data are needed about non-tenure-track faculty. A systematic national dataset needs to be designed with all types of faculty in mind. With the ending of the National Studies of Postsecondary Faculty (NSOPF), it is important to have a continuing source of data that examine and categorize non-tenure-track faculty. Institutions need to establish more robust systems internally to collect information about non-tenure-track faculty, particularly differences by contract and discipline. Further studies on non-tenure-track faculty should also take into consideration the different functional typologies of non-tenure-track faculty and find ways of incorporating them into their samples as well as interpreting the data.

Non-tenure-track faculty currently account for a majority of the faculty in higher education. If the past thirty years are any indication of a trend, they will continue to play a large role in institutions of higher education. Nevertheless, most institutions have failed to incorporate long-term policies for non-tenure-track faculty. Stakeholders in institutions of higher education need to develop long-term strategies regarding non-tenure-track faculty, depending on the context of the institutions. Issues such as hiring practices, reappointment, compensation, benefits, work responsibilities, governance, and promotion should be addressed explicitly in an overall institutional faculty plan and carried out consistently.

The research on non-tenure-track faculty could be theorized in more meaningful ways to best capture the faculty experience as a hybrid of professional and laborer.

Research can apply theories from other disciplines such as political science or organizational studies to further explore the role of non-tenure-track faculty and their effect on higher education. Researchers can better understand non-tenure-track faculty by using a multidisciplinary perspective that incorporates insights from economics, sociology, psychology, and labor relations.

Misconceptions and stereotypes about non-tenure-track faculty, whether positive or negative, do not serve the population well because they do not provide accurate information that is needed to inform policies and practices that benefit both the faculty and the institution. Studies that move away from a deficit perspective can provide us a new way of understanding non-tenure-track faculty and enhance our knowledge. Studies should examine the positive features of the non-tenure-track faculty experience such as love of teaching, program environment, appreciation for academia, work with students, service to society, and fulfillment of personal priorities. Instead of ideology, empirical data about non-tenure-track faculty should drive policy and practice. These data include evidence suggesting that they lack basic necessities to complete their work, are as committed as tenure-track faculty, and are not paid for office hours at most institutions.

Many recommendations for improving working conditions for non-tenure-track faculty have been highly generalized and have not examined site-specific changes needed in programs, departments, colleges, and universities. Although global plans and ideas for professionalizing non-tenure-track faculty have been extremely helpful, they also have masked important variations that leaders should take into consideration as they institutionalize change. To move forward, solutions need to take into account the institutional context and different typology of non-tenure-track faculty to provide solutions that better serve different groups in different institutions. It is necessary to inform other institutions through more case study research and examples of institutions that have altered their policies and practices. This monograph provides a needed synthesis of the existing literature and advice for practitioners trying to define policies and practices for non-tenure-track faculty, policymakers attempting to understand the empirical research available to inform their decisions, and researchers seeking to conduct research on non-tenure-track faculty.

Given the large amount of data that must be synthesized to develop an accurate portrait, the authors dedicated this monograph to expand on the topic of non-tenure-track faculty; building on their earlier work in volume 36, issue number 4 of ASHE Higher Education Report, *Understanding the New Majority of Non-Tenure-Track Faculty in Higher Education: Demographics, Experiences, and Plans of Action* (referenced in upcoming chapters).

Foreword

The typical scenario goes something like this: A well-paid senior faculty member leaves the institution, hiring freezes (or other cost-saving measures) prevent replacement of the faculty member, and a new Ph.D. who recently moved to the area is hired at a fraction of the salary of the recently resigned professor. The plan is to hire the non-tenure-track faculty member for a short-term, one-year appointment to address immediate teaching needs. The intention was (and is) to replace the senior faculty member, but the budget crisis prevents such action. When it comes time to make permanent budget cuts to meet shortfalls, the faculty line is cut, leaving in its wake unmet teaching and advising needs and a temporary non-tenure-track employee to fill the gap.

Such a scenario has become the norm on many campuses as faculty and administrators deal with the best way to handle the budget crisis facing many colleges and universities. The salary savings created by hiring freezes are easy targets for cutting budgets. As Kezar and Sam astutely point out, "Market logic [becomes] more important than educational goals," resulting in shifts in the academic labor force. Decisions about faculty hires are often made mindful of the financial bottom line without acknowledging or being able to reconcile the impact these decisions have on students, departmental health, or faculty composition. Every decision made about faculty has a consequence, even if it is often overlooked and not fully recognized. This monograph sheds light on the topic of non-tenure-track faculty, expanding on Kezar and Sam's earlier research found in volume 36, issue number 4 of ASHE Higher Education

Report, *Understanding the New Majority of Non-Tenure-Track Faculty in Higher Education: Demographics, Experiences, and Plans of Action.*

As editors, we thought it important to capture the landscape of non-tenure-track faculty—as the authors do in volume 36, issue number 4—as well as examine the underlying ideologies and theories that have shaped decision making in the past and then use these same theoretical lenses to provide readers with sound and practical recommendations to shape the future, as the authors do here in this monograph.

Faculty work does not operate independently of context, nor is it something that is experienced homogeneously. Just as traditional tenure-track faculty are a very diverse group demographically and professionally, so are non-tenure-track faculty. In this regard, Kezar and Sam's monograph on theories and tensions is a companion to other Jossey-Bass ASHE monographs that have examined the pipelines, contexts, and constructs associated with faculty work. For example, Susan Gardner in *The Development of Doctoral Students: Phases of Challenge and Support* looks critically at doctoral student development and the pipeline of prospective faculty. Just as faculty have multiple and complex career desires, so too do graduate students. In their monograph, *Faculty Careers and Work Lives: A Professional Growth Perspective,* authors KerryAnn O'Meara, Aimee LaPointe Terosky, and Anna Neumann provide a holistic view of faculty development. Although they do not focus on non-tenure-track faculty, their perspective does call for a broad examination of the context of faculty work for tenure- and non-tenure-track faculty. The monograph by Barbara Townsend and Susan Twombly, *Community College Faculty: Overlooked and Undervalued,* although limited to the community college context, is also relevant because the community college context is one with a disproportionate number of non-tenure-track faculty. Collectively these monographs provide readers with a broad understanding of the background, history, pipeline, demographics, context, and theoretical concepts that guide understanding about tenure- and non-tenure-track faculty life.

The intent of the ASHE monograph series is to provide readers a synthesis and critical analysis of current issues in higher education as presented in the literature. The goal is to help guide informed practice and relevant research for researchers and practitioners. When it comes to the topic of non-tenure-track faculty, Kezar and Sam provide a very nuanced, thorough, critical, and useful analysis of the complex milieu of non-tenure-track faculty.

Kelly Ward
Series Editor

Acknowledgments

We would like to thank and dedicate this book to the many non-tenure-track faculty leaders who spoke with us these last two years while engaging in a national study on this important topic as well as those working toward positive solutions. We also wish to thank the editors of this series and the reviewers for their helpful feedback to make the monograph an even stronger contribution.

Cecile Sam would like to thank her family for their love and support and her friends for their kindness and patience.

Published online in Wiley Online Library
(wileyonlinelibrary.com) • DOI: 10.1002/aehe.3605

Introduction and Overview

Academic tenure is too prevalent a practice to disappear and too
consequential a policy to disregard.

—Chait and Ford, 1982, ix

THESE WORDS ARE NOW QUITE IRONIC in a world where tenure
has been in significant decline and the workforce is changing to a largely
non-tenure-track faculty. The shift in the composition of faculty has received
limited attention until recently.[1] In the last five years, a few books have doc-
umented this demographic shift, most prominently Schuster and Finkelstein's
The American Faculty: The Restructuring of Academic Work and Careers (2006a).
Although early books tried to bring visibility to part-time and full-time non-
tenure-track faculty, who were largely ignored in the academy, these books
were developed before the increase in part-time numbers and rise of full-time
non-tenure-track faculty (Gappa and Leslie, 1993; Baldwin and Chronister,
2001). Through these initial texts as well as greater awareness on individual
campuses, people are beginning to recognize the major change in faculty composition that has taken place. We know little, however, about the implications
of this change. Several researchers who have analyzed or explored non-tenure-
track faculty have done so from focused perspectives, examining the growing
numbers (Schuster and Finkelstein, 2006a; Gappa and Leslie, 1993; Baldwin
and Chronister, 2001; Hollenshead and others, 2007), the reasons for the
growth in non-tenure-track faculty (Cross and Goldenberg, 2003), or the experience of being a non-tenure-track faculty member (Baldwin and Chronister,
2001; Gappa and Leslie, 1993; Schell and Stock, 2001). A few texts take a

comprehensive view (Gappa and Leslie, 1993, and Baldwin and Chronister, 2001, are the major exceptions) and examine a plethora of topics: the reasons for growth, the expectations of non-tenure-track faculty, the nature of work role and career trajectories, and policies and practices institutions can implement that can improve the working conditions for non-tenure-track faculty. Furthermore, because the landscape is changing rapidly, these texts are becoming outdated. We build on these two important texts by examining new research on the effect of non-tenure-track faculty on the academy, discussing rising tensions in the empirical research, and synthesizing the significant empirical literature to date.

Need for the Monograph

Much of the literature about non-tenure-track faculty has been ideologically driven and attempts to either portray these faculty as destroying the integrity of the academic environment and threatening tenure or to demonstrate the oppression of the faculty experience and demonstrate how non-tenure-track faculty represent the inequities and problems of the academy. Certainly exceptions exist such as the data-driven work by Schuster and Finkelstein (2006a), Baldwin and Chronister (2001), and Gappa and Leslie (1993). This monograph takes a more balanced approach, looking at the pros and cons and at the complexities of the lives of non-tenure-track faculty and the implications of this workforce for the academy. A more balanced and holistic perspective helps policymakers and campus leaders to make better decisions about their campuses. We present all perspectives, as no book so far has brought together both ideological and data-driven perspectives in one place.

Moreover, because of the nature of empirical research and the specificity that it requires, it is difficult to obtain a bird's-eye view of non-tenure-track faculty. Many of the texts on non-tenure-track faculty focus only on part-time faculty (Gappa and Leslie, 1993) or only on full-time non-tenure-track faculty (Baldwin and Chronister, 2001). Much of the literature also does not recognize disciplinary differences or differences by institutional type. The working conditions, policies, solutions, and experience of non-tenure-track faculty vary vastly by work status (part time or full time), discipline, and institutional type.

Furthermore, the presence of unions on campus also makes a difference in the experiences and working conditions of faculty. This monograph is sensitive to these types of differences that are often overlooked or fragmented in the literature.

Why is understanding non-tenure-track faculty so important? They are the most common appointments, with three out of every four being off the tenure track—part and full time (Schuster and Finkelstein, 2006a; Forrest Cataldi, Fahimi, and Bradburn, 2005). Certainly their sheer numbers suggest that we need to understand more about them and their impact on the academy. More important, the main contribution of this monograph and reason for exploring non-tenure-track faculty is that we can no longer continue to operate according to the *perceived* status quo, pretending that tenured faculty are the mainline faculty of the academy. This reality has come to pass in the last twenty years, and campus leaders, faculty, staff, students, policymakers, and the general public should realize that we need more intentional planning and analysis of this new workforce—or, as some suggest, we need to revisit the value of tenure. Will we make the non-tenure-track faculty route a professional, recognized, and rewarding career option? Will we revisit faculty roles more generally?

Many campuses across the country have done little to change their policies and practices to acknowledge and professionalize the non-tenure-track faculty. Campuses lack a general awareness of the large growth of numbers. Those campuses that are slowly becoming aware of the growth are struggling to understand new policies and practices that can be put in place (and have long and extended campus discussions about whether *any* should be put in place). The most important reason for understanding and examining non-tenure-track faculty, however, is that they teach the majority of students in higher education; thus, they are key to creating the teaching and learning environment. They are in large measure the individuals responsible for meeting the primary mission of postsecondary institutions, and to know so little about who these faculty are (and how to support them) is at best reckless and at worst unethical. Faculty work conditions, many argue, are related to student learning conditions (Benjamin, 2002, 2003a, 2003b; Kezar and Sam, 2009; Curtis and Jacobe, 2006; Umbach, 2007). Understanding the experience and impact of non-tenure-track faculty is important to identify policies needed to refashion the academy. A fundamental change in the workforce has occurred, but the understanding of this shift is limited.

Purpose and Audience

Our overarching goal in this monograph is to fill the void in the literature that lacks a meta-analysis of the research about non-tenure-track faculty. The existing research is difficult to wade through; it is produced by many groups with differing agendas and focused on varying goals and facets of the non-tenure-track issue. Thus, our first goal is to synthesize and analyze the research that is available to provide the reader a better understanding of this new majority. Another major purpose of meta-analysis is to critique the literature and to help find new directions for research and practice. In reviewing the research on non-tenure-track faculty, we realized that they have been conceptualized and theorized in limited ways. Our second goal is to make visible the underlying ideologies and assumptions and to help dispel misconceptions. In addition, meta-analysis can help provide direction for practice through patterns and themes in the literature. By having a comprehensive source of the research and literature on non-tenure-track faculty, we hope to lay down the foundation for reasoned, intelligent, and ethical dialogue among stakeholders in the academy that will lead to changing the status quo that currently is not serving students or the general public.

Terminology

We refer to this growing new profile of faculty as *nontenure track* for both part-time and full-time appointments that are ineligible for tenure review. We believe it is important to have an umbrella term to refer to this large population and to examine some similarities individuals off the tenure track share. We acknowledge that using only the term *non-tenure-track faculty* to describe the entire population of faculty not on the tenure track lacks precision, as members of this group vary tremendously. One major difference referred to in the literature is part time versus full time. We refer to part-time and full-time non-tenure-track faculty throughout the monograph to point out important differences in these groups, but we point out that the plethora of terms that have emerged have caused tremendous confusion, and we avoid using the alphabet soup of names that have emerged: contingent, lecturer, instructor, clinical faculty, adjunct, and more. Terminology is one of the most difficult conundrums of recognizing and understanding non-tenure-track faculty. Most terms for this group of faculty reflect a particular element of focus (lecturer) that they teach or amount of teaching (part time), but these terms do not comprehensively reflect their status. Given the vast number of names in the literature, we wanted some clear terminology to break this confusion; thus, our umbrella term when we refer to similarities these groups share is "nontenure track." When meaningful differences exist, they usually reflect the part-time and full-time contract status, so we use these two terms when they are relevant to identify significant differences in these groups.

Although we use the term *nontenure track,* other groups have gravitated toward the word *contingent* because it reflects the precarious nature of the contracts of part-time and full-time non-tenure-track faculty (the National Education Association and the American Federation of Teachers, for example). Even among the faculty, conflicts exist related to terminology, with some terms being more preferred than others. For example, some faculty find the word "adjunct" to describe faculty who teach part time distasteful, while others do not mind. We recognize that these terms are value laden and problematic. The evolution of these terms is hard to trace, but what is important to understand is that more than fifty terms exist for non-tenure-track faculty and that in recent years an effort has been made to narrow the terminology and to come up with more precise and standard terminology. We follow this practice of standardizing language in this monograph while respecting a major difference in employment—full and part time.

Although we need some term to refer to this growing group of faculty—in our case *nontenure track*—we are clear throughout the monograph to break out studies and research specific to part-time and full-time non-tenure-track faculty when such a designation is made. Many studies have not broken down the research and disaggregated these groups, but when studies are specific to these populations, we note this information. We seek to make the trends about full-time and part-time faculty clear to readers, but because many researchers have not studied these groups separately, we are not always able to make these distinctions. It is important to note that part-time faculty are represented more in community colleges and in certain disciplines such as law. Full-time non-tenure-track faculty are represented more in four-year institutions and in certain disciplines such as mathematics. However, it is important to note that non-tenure-track faculty are shaped by institutional type and discipline. These structures play a major role in the experiences, commitment, and plans of action of non-tenure-track faculty.

It is also important to note one methodological issue related to terminology. Some of the studies we report on focus only on part-time non-tenure-track faculty. When we report these data, we use the term "part time" rather than "nontenure track" to make the reader understand that the study was limited to a subsection of non-tenure-track faculty. Other studies have looked exclusively at full-time non-tenure-track faculty, and another set of studies does not differentiate the two but has grouped together part time and full time or is unclear about the exact population. Less than one-tenth of part-time faculty have tenure; these groups have not been studied separately and are usually included with part-time non-tenure-track faculty. Where we have clarity, we make specific note; otherwise, we use the generic term to refer to non-tenure-track part-time faculty.

We would like to remind readers that, first and foremost, we are talking about faculty in higher education. We call people back to referring to all faculty as "the faculty." Making the majority of faculty take on a potentially negative or misleading label in the long run is likely to create more problems. In the short run, we do need to understand that the faculty is an incredibly diverse group with many different contracts, and we need to better understand the current distinctions so we can develop the best staffing arrangements for different campuses and institutions. But ultimately we argue that it is in the best interests of higher education to conceptualize the faculty as a single and united group, even if individual members of the group have different contracts.

Related to the notion of returning to a single term for the faculty, we also think it is important to think about the non-tenure-track faculty as part of the larger issue of defining the profession of faculty or staffing and human resources for higher education. It may be that people are reluctant to think about faculty hiring as a staffing or human resource issue because that term is associated with administrative actions and behavior. For those more comfortable with the term "profession" than "human resources," it is critical that faculty take more responsibility for who is part of the profession, who is teaching courses, who is creating a learning environment for students, and what it means to be a scholar, academic, and faculty member. Because tenure-track faculty have largely abdicated their role in defining the professoriate (some might argue that hiring decisions were taken away from the faculty during the corporatization of higher education), non-tenure-track faculty float along without a professional anchor or career route (Burgan, 2006). In the absence of the tenure-track faculty's defining what it means to be a professional without tenure, administrators have claimed this space, providing new types of contracts but minimal policies and procedures. But in large measure, few faculty or administrators have been thinking intentionally about bringing non-tenure-track faculty into the faculty profession and how they fit into the larger human resource and staffing arrangements for higher education. Our point is not to take sides about whether this is an issue of professionalization or academic staffing but to suggest that the question of non-tenure-track faculty is likely one that is best made in relationship to thinking about total faculty/staffing for the campus.

Background: Understanding the Conflicting Research

Scholars and writers about non-tenure-track faculty agree on few issues, with the exceptions that non-tenure-track faculty now constitute two-thirds of the faculty (with non-tenure-track full-time faculty being one-third of full-time faculty) and that their numbers have been rising significantly in the last two decades. After that well-documented fact, research evidence about non-tenure-track faculty is mixed, and interpretations of data are often one-sided, not examining alternative explanations. In writing this monograph, we undertake a great challenge because several conditions make it very difficult to clearly understand the background, experience, and effect of non-tenure-track faculty. Simple questions like: Are non-tenure-track faculty satisfied? result in complex answers with little agreement among studies. Why such a confused landscape? We suggest that five primary conditions make the study of non-tenure-track faculty complex: ideology, theory, data sources, heterogeneity of the group, and a historical and contextual view.

Ideology

Researchers studying or writing about non-tenure-track faculty have generally adopted two different ideologies. Scholars maintaining the first perspective focus on non-tenure-track faculty and the exploitation that occurs—low salaries, minimal benefits, and a lack of job security. Unions and non-tenure-track faculty (especially those in humanities and liberal arts) generally hold this position. The same authors often believe that non-tenure-track faculty are a threat to tenure and traditional academic staffing arrangements. Scholars maintaining the second perspective focus on the non-tenure-track faculty path as allowing career flexibility, particularly for women, see it as a way to bring in expertise to the institution, and believe that it is important to improve the working conditions for these faculty as they that have grown in numbers. Administrators but also some faculty in professional fields and those who are disillusioned with tenure often hold this perspective. A third, less mentioned perspective blends the two ideologies, acknowledging the exploitation of some and the choice of others. Some non-tenure-track faculty in certain fields (English composition, for example) are being exploited and at only some campuses. Other non-tenure-track faculty have chosen this route and view it as an alternative to tenure. For them, tenure is a less desirable option because of the overly long working hours to produce research for tenure and promotion, which is often inhospitable to faculty with families.

These deeply ingrained perspectives affect people's interpretation of the data and the way they write about non-tenure-track faculty. Different people look at the same data and arrive at different conclusions. This phenomenon is similar to other controversial issues such as climate change, where ideology can make understanding the data extremely difficult. Data need to be interpreted, and the lenses people bring sway their views. Contested issues often have more varied interpretations and make consensus difficult. As noted earlier, these perspectives are often related to one's position as a tenure-track or non-tenure-track faculty, administrator, or union member.

Theory

Another issue that affects our understanding of non-tenure-track faculty is the theories (or lack of theories) brought to bear. Much of the research conducted is atheoretical and does not draw on known concepts about labor markets, contingent labor, work motivation, and non-tenure-track professionals. When theory is used, it draws from only a few disciplines—economic theories, sociological theories, psychological theories, and labor relations theories (see "Theories Used to Study and Understand Non-Tenure-Track Faculty" later in this monograph). In terms of economic theories, dual market, supply and demand, underemployment, risk taking, and social exchange have been applied focusing on general patterns in the economy, workforce restructuring, or contracts (Cross and Goldenberg, 2009; Ehrenberg and Zhang, 2004, 2005; Toutkoushian and Bellas, 2003; Umbach, 2007). Sociological theories of the political economy examine how academic capitalism has come to prevail on college campuses, making market logic more important than educational goals and resulting in the deprofessionalization and deskilling of faculty—losing their tenure status and becoming managed professionals under their non-tenure-track status (Rhoades, 1996). Psychological theories such as commitment theory, person-job fit, and faculty growth and development look more at how individuals make choices and variations in satisfaction and impact (Bland and others 2006; Maynard and Joseph, 2008; O'Meara, Terosky, and Neumann, 2008). Labor relations studies examine the way faculty can mobilize to create changes in working conditions and the role of unions. Organizational theory has been used fewer times and more tacitly than other theories, though exceptions exist such as Gappa and Leslie's work (1993) examining organizational concepts. All these theories have important insights to offer, but typically studies have applied a single economic, sociological, or psychological lens. Like the understanding of climate change, understanding non-tenure-track faculty may require an inter-disciplinary perspective that draws together these various conceptual lenses.

Lack of Meaningful Data

Various researchers have noted the difficulty in accessing meaningful data about non-tenure-track faculty (Chait and Ford, 1982; Cross and Goldenberg, 2009). Researchers point to the challenge of even identifying non-tenure-track faculty because the names and labels used for non-tenure-track faculty vary by institution. Published lists of titles demonstrate close to fifty different terms used to identify part-time non-tenure-track faculty alone (Berry, 2005). As a result, studies typically miss many of the faculty based only on identification and terminology. Moreover at the institutional level, many non-tenure-track faculty, especially part-time faculty, are hired by departments from semester to semester; thus, the statistics and data change so rapidly that it is difficult for institutional research offices to sort out how many and what type of non-tenure-track faculty are hired. In a study of ten elite research universities (Cross and Goldenberg, 2009), none of the institutions could easily come up with data about the non-tenure-track faculty. Some states have better sources of data about employment and contracts than others, making available data uneven and not comparable. But because institutional data are often inaccurate, state-level data likely lack accuracy as well. At the federal level, the National Study of Postsecondary Faculty (NSOPF) was one of the best sources of data about non-tenure-track faculty, but the survey was originally designed with tenure-track faculty largely in mind and has not always captured the experience and background of non-tenure-track faculty as sharply.

Unfortunately, the National Center for Education Statistics has decided it will no longer fund the NSOPF database, limiting any further research on faculty. The last national survey was in 2004. The Higher Education Research Institute (HERI) at the University of California, Los Angeles, also conducts regular national faculty surveys, every three years. In 2007–08, it added more questions to specifically explore the non-tenure-track faculty experience. Like the NSOPF, the survey was originally designed for tenure-track faculty and is still largely targeted toward tenure-track faculty. The survey sample also contains few community colleges but has grown in number in the last two cycles. Moreover, the HERI database is proprietary, and access is limited to those with the ability to pay. With limited data sources, researchers often conduct local and individual studies with smaller samples that are more feasible, but results are difficult to generalize.

Heterogeneity

Another issue that makes interpretation and conclusions difficult is that non-tenure-track faculty are heterogeneous. Some studies have assumed that non-tenure-track faculty were a homogeneous group and conducted large-scale surveys, making generalizations across vastly different faculty with different motivations, experiences, contracts, working conditions, disciplinary backgrounds, and institutional types (Bland and others, 2006; Jacoby, 2006; Umbach, 2007; Jaeger and Eagan, 2009; Eagan and Jaeger, 2009; Banachowski, 1996). Our review of the research demonstrates that the heterogeneous nature of non-tenure-track faculty is extremely meaningful to understanding their experience (see Kezar and Sam, 2010, for more on the differences of non-tenure-track faculty by discipline and institutional types). Only by examining and disaggregating non-tenure-track faculty into subgroups can we truly understand their satisfaction, experience, and potentially their impact on higher education.

Historical and Contextual Analysis

Historical and social forces also shape our understanding of non-tenure-track faculty; we can achieve greater understanding by looking at them in the broader context of higher education and the changes that have been occurring. It is important to recognize that certain historical markers can help us to understand how we ended up with the current staffing patterns and demonstrate ways that we might alter and create better professional circumstances for faculty. For example, the rapid rise in full-time non-tenure-track faculty happened just after higher education came under critical attack in the late 1980s for largely abandoning undergraduate education. Studies and reports demonstrated that teaching assistants, not tenure-track faculty, were teaching introductory courses, particularly at large institutions (*Involvement in Learning*, 1985). National reports critiqued campuses for not focusing on undergraduate education, which policymakers and taxpayers felt was a priority. Tenured faculty did not offer to teach introductory courses or change the nature of their work, so campuses turned to non-tenure-track faculty instead of teaching assistants. The general public did not understand that these new faculty were not the same as tenure-track faculty, but the public did understand that they were not teaching assistants. These broader historical trends help us to comprehend how we might rethink our current approach to staffing.

Introduction to the Players: Groups Studying Non-Tenure-Track Faculty

To understand the landscape of non-tenure-track faculty, it helps to be introduced to various players who have written about and created policy related to non-tenure-track faculty. The first group to write about non-tenure-track faculty were higher education scholars such as Leslie, Kellams, and Gunne (1982), Gappa and Leslie (1993), Bowen and Schuster (1986), and other scholars documenting changes in community college in the 1970s. The studies largely examined the rising numbers, examined the experiences and motivations of non-tenure-track faculty, primarily part-time faculty, and pointed out how these faculty were largely invisible, even as their numbers were growing. The research often focused on community colleges, as the emergence of part-time faculty happened to a greater degree in these institutions early in the 1970s and 1980s.

The rise in full-time non-tenure-track positions happened later in the 1990s. The Faculty Forum on Roles and Rewards of the American Association for Higher Education (AAHE) was formed in the 1990s and began to address the issues of non-tenure-track faculty, the changing nature of tenure, and the changing faculty. The forum focused more on the issue of full-time non-tenure-track faculty at four-year institutions—the emerging issue in the 1990s among AAHE members. One of the major projects that emerged out of the forum, the New Pathways Project, looked at a variety of alternatives to tenured positions as currently conceptualized. Driven by research that demonstrated that women and faculty of color often found tenure-track positions unwelcoming, the forum explored other avenues such as teaching-only tenure-track lines or nontenured faculty positions. The forum was also responding to Boyer's *Scholarship Reconsidered: Priorities of the Professoriate* (1990), which raised concerns about the narrow ways that faculty scholarship and life have been conceived, trying to broaden the perspective of faculty on the tenure-track career, largely focused on research over teaching and pure research rather than applied research.

In the late 1990s, many other groups began to recognize the large numbers of non-tenure-track faculty in the academy and to see the rise as problematic

(Schell and Stock, 2001). In particular, various disciplinary societies began to address and conduct research on non-tenure-track faculty (for example, the *2002 AHA–OAH Survey of Part-time and Adjunct Faculty* and the *2000 Report of the Ad Hoc Committee on Priorities and Problems of the American Philosophical Association*). Liberal arts disciplines with high numbers of non-tenure-track faculty were the most active, including composition and history. Several of the disciplinary societies began to work on policy statements related to the use of non-tenure-track faculty and established a coalition across several disciplines that have high concentrations of non-tenure-track faculty: the Coalition on the Academic Workforce (Schell and Stock, 2001). Surprisingly, many fields that have larger numbers of non-tenure-track faculty such as law, medicine, and education were not actively involved in advocating for or researching non-tenure-track faculty. One of the major differences noted in the literature between these groups is that non-tenure-track faculty in vocational and professional areas often have other employment and are not interested in full-time employment in the academy. The research emerging from the disciplines adds a new perspective because it is conducted by non-tenure-track faculty themselves. Other studies conducted by tenure-track faculty have sometimes been biased against non-tenure-track faculty or misunderstood their experience and working conditions (described in detail in the chapters on applied theories and tensions in the research).

During the mid- to late 1990s, unions began to recognize, write about, and research non-tenure-track faculty. The American Association of University Professors (AAUP), the National Education Association (NEA), and the American Federation of Teachers (AFT) developed subgroups to work on policy statements related to non-tenure-track faculty. Each organization developed a report based on research advocating for certain changes in policies and practices on campus (see, for example, *Standards of Good Practice in the Employment of Full-Time Non-Tenure-Track Faculty: Professionals and Colleagues* [AFT Higher Education, 2005]). The AFT recently published (2010) a national survey of the experience and background of non-tenure-track faculty. The NEA conducted national focus groups with non-tenure-track faculty in 2008 and 2009 and plans a national survey in 2010. The unions also carried out smaller-scale research efforts in the early 2000s. In addition, state and regional union groups became prominent in California, Illinois, Massachusetts, and Wisconsin, creating listservs, Web sites, and resources to help mobilize and support non-tenure-track faculty.

As an alternative to unions, other professional groups have begun to emerge from a growing number of non-tenure-track faculty leaders. These groups help provide support for non-tenure-track faculty, especially those in states that are unable to unionize. For example, Adjunct Nation has produced a series of publications such as the *Adjunct Advocate* to help non-tenure-track faculty (with an emphasis on part-time faculty) deal with challenging working conditions and provide a space for both mobilization and an exchange of ideas. Another group, the New Faculty Majority, aims to create a unified front across all disciplines and groups and to provide a united voice when speaking to legislators and policymakers.

Some states have also engaged in research on non-tenure-track faculty based on reports of inequitable treatment. For example, the state of Illinois in 2005 conducted a study examining the use and deployment of non-tenure-track faculty and found that their working conditions were not equitable with other faculty. California and New Mexico have also conducted studies of non-tenure-track faculty to examine whether states should recommend or encourage institutional policies and practices to better serve non-tenure-track faculty. In the future, we imagine more states will conduct research on non-tenure-track faculty, as non-tenure-track faculty are appealing more to legislatures related to their working conditions because they feel that higher education administrators or policymakers have been unresponsive to their concerns.

Higher education associations have also conducted research on non-tenure-track faculty; for example, the Association of American Universities (AAU) conducted a study of major research universities and their deployment of non-tenure-track faculty (2001), examining baseline data and recommending some best practices related to the use of non-tenure-track faculty. The American Council on Education (ACE) developed a publication using national data describing the rising trend, background, and experience of non-tenure-track faculty (Anderson, 2002). But the national higher education organizations have conducted less research than expected for such a significant national topic.

Each of these groups has different vested interests, which affect the way they study and describe the experience, working conditions, deployment, and impact of non-tenure-track faculty. Even the language they use and the focus they take to study the issue suggest a different vested interest. The AAU (2001) and the ACE (1981), for example, focus on the deployment and best use of both full-time and part-time non-tenure-track faculty as part of an overall human resource scheme, flexibility, and cost savings. Non-tenure-track faculty are more likely to study the experience and working conditions of non-tenure-track faculty in an effort to demonstrate problems that they themselves have experienced. Each perspective sheds light on the issue, but similar to the theories, they tend to shine only partial light. Looking across the perspectives can help enhance our knowledge. These various groups also represent sources of bias in interpretation that need to be recognized as well.

Although we cannot pretend to be free of any perspective, our goal in reviewing the research has been to be open to differing perspectives and to present multiple views. Yet we acknowledge we hold some basic assumptions. Non-tenure-track faculty will likely be part of academic institutions in the future and in large numbers. Their current treatment at many institutions does not fall in line with best organizational practices. We think that there are ways to incorporate non-tenure-track faculty into the academy that can serve to strengthen higher education. Although we think that tenure is a valuable structure, it may not be desirable in all circumstances, and we think that tenure reforms should be debated and considered. Although our perspective may be apparent in some of our discussion, we hope that the meta-analysis reflects a range of views and helps people consider multiple alternatives.

Organization of the Monograph

This monograph complements volume 36, issue number 4 of ASHE Higher Education Report: *Understanding the New Majority of Non-Tenure-Track Faculty*, and offocuses on theories applied to study non-tenure-track faculty and philosophical and practical tensions represented in the literature.

The next chapter, "Theories Used to Study and Understand Non-Tenure-Track Faculty," reviews theories applied to the study of these faculty. As studies became more sophisticated and began examining issues such as faculty productivity, commitment, and outcomes, researchers also looked for analytic lenses to understand the behavior of non-tenure-track faculty. The critical message from this chapter is that we need insights from a variety of disciplines and theories to truly understand non-tenure-track faculty. At this time, we lack the sophisticated application of theories to understand this emerging group of faculty.

The following chapter, "Tensions," examines the various conflicts that arise in ideology, practice, and empirical research regarding non-tenure-track faculty and their role in the academy. It begins with a discussion of the role of non-tenure-track faculty in relation to tenure and then discusses the tension in the two-tier system between tenure-track and non-tenure-track faculty (Tolbert, 1998; Hough, 2003), and competing interests (Haeger, 1998; Hough, 2003; Dyer-Witheford, 2005). Both theories and tensions examine underlying beliefs and assumptions critical for shaping policy and conceptualizing research. The chapter focuses on these underlying beliefs as they have remained tacit and, we argue, have negatively affected current policies for non-tenure-track faculty. By making these assumptions explicit, we hope to change the nature of the dialogue and resulting policies. The chapter ends with a review of the research on productivity, cost-effectiveness, student outcomes, and the effects of the rising number of non-tenure-track faculty, systematically addressing various tensions in the literature that have not been brought together and examined as a whole. More productive policymaking regarding non-tenure-track faculty will likely be facilitated with productive discussion and understanding of this group.

The final chapter, "Conclusion and Suggestions for Further Research," offers conclusions related to research from earlier chapters and provides ideas for future research.

In the end, we are trying to address the important questions and their elusive answers, such as to what extent institutions should rely on non-tenure-track faculty, how can colleges and universities employ these individuals in a way that is fair to the entire faculty, how can faculty be organized so as to strengthen institutional capacity to meet their missions of teaching students and advancing knowledge, and how to address quality issues that emerge because of the change in faculty? As Schuster and Finkelstein (2006a) note, a revolution has taken place among faculty, and it would be irresponsible not to better understand this issue. Now that a body of research has been amassed, we have taken on the task of organizing and synthesizing this research to try to answer these questions and to propose future research that will help us address these questions.

Our meta-analysis relies heavily on three comprehensive studies: *The Invisible Faculty: Improving the Status of Part-Timers in Higher Education* (Gappa and Leslie, 1993), focused exclusively on part-time faculty; *Teaching Without Tenure* (Baldwin and Chronister, 2001), focused on full-time non-tenure-track faculty; and *Making the Best of Both Worlds* (Hollenshead and others, 2007), which is the only national study looking at all non-tenure-track faculty in four-year institutions. *The Invisible Faculty* is a qualitative case study of multiple institutions examining policies and practices related to part-time faculty— hiring, salary, benefits, governance. Gappa and Leslie interviewed administrators and tenure-track faculty about their views of part-time faculty and talked to part-time faculty about their experiences. *Teaching Without Tenure* is also a qualitative case study of multiple institutions examining policies and practices related to full-time non-tenure-track faculty. It was the first major study to focus on this growing population. The book ranges in topics from the history and reasons for growth to reports about policies and practices used on campuses to a report of the experiences of full-time non-tenure-track faculty. *Making the Best of Both Worlds* is a national quantitative study of approximately 500 institutions asking administrators about their deployment, policies, and practices relative to both part-time and full-time non-tenure-track faculty. It is one of the few studies to disaggregate these groups in studies and examine differences in policy.

In volume 36, issue number 4 of ASHE Higher Education Report, Kezar and Sam also cover other important topics focused on the demographics, historical developments, experiences and outcomes of non-tenure-track faculty as compared with those of tenured or tenure-track faculty.

Theories Used to Study and Understand Non-Tenure-Track Faculty

Concerns about the effects of part-time teaching on quality education often turn into critiques of part-time faculty as individuals or as a class of undifferentiated faculty—a problematic rhetorical move that shifts responsibilities from institutions to individuals who occupy the problematic positions.

—Schell and Stock, 2001, p. 326

THEORIES USED TO CONCEPTUALIZE non-tenure-track faculty significantly impact the research and assumptions brought to bear on this topic. Theories are also important for understanding and explaining the trends found in existing data (reviewed in Kezar and Sam, 2010). This chapter reviews theories that have been applied to the study of non-tenure-track faculty to chart how they have been conceptualized, to document underlying assumptions and beliefs, and to explore whether other theories might help better explain their behavior and experience.

As noted in the previous chapter, researchers use theories from four main social science disciplines to explain and explore the behavior and working conditions of non-tenure-track faculty: economic theories, sociological theories, psychological theories, and labor relations theories. At present, the application of theory is uneven. Some theories have helped shed light on the topic of non-tenure-track faculty, while others seem inaccurate or lack a strong fit. This chapter provides an overview of theories used, highlighting some promising directions such as professionalization theory, underemployment theory, mobilization theory, and agency theory. It also critiques the use of inappropriate theories that bring in fundamental assumptions that are a weak fit for studying non-tenure-track faculty. For example, a differentiating assumption in these theories is whether non-tenure-track faculty are laborers or professionals. Is their behavior driven by the code or norms of other contingent labor in the business world or the norms of the academy? Can changes in employment contracts sufficiently alter socialization patterns learned from graduate school? Although scholars using these theories tend not to focus on these questions, we think these questions reveal important underlying assumptions and help identify pertinent theories. The conceptualization of faculty as laborers or professionals makes a big difference in understanding their behavior and effect.

Another issue is the tendency for the focus of studies to be too narrow because of the use of a single disciplinary perspective. These theories act as lenses that focus our attention on particular elements at the cost of paying attention to other elements. For instance, to understand non-tenure-track faculty only in economic terms means that it is difficult to see the organizational effect faculty may have. Likewise, scholars have yet to apply numerous theories in the various disciplines (such as intergroup contact theory or actor network theory) to non-tenure-track faculty, although they have the potential to expand our understanding. Our contention is that by juxtaposing these various disciplines and theories, we can better understand how we come to know non-tenure-track faculty and how we can begin to know them further. The chapter begins by reviewing theories in these four disciplines.

Economic Theories

Economic theories are primarily used to understand the behavior and impact of non-tenure-track faculty members. Labor economists have looked at the contingent[2] workforce and working arrangements of other professions, and higher education scholars have adopted these perspectives to understand non-tenure-track faculty in the academy, particularly dual-market theory. Dual-market theory documents the segmentation of the labor market into a primary market (tenure track) and secondary market (nontenure track), with each market operating with different principles and rules (Doeringer and Piore, 1971; Shaker, 2008; Youn, 1988). Primary markets offer security, health benefits, and other privileges, while secondary markets offer less security and fewer benefits. To compete globally, companies began to downsize and restructure, adding a second contingent workforce. The oversupply of individuals with doctorates in the 1970s set up a situation for a secondary workforce to emerge.

Economists suggest that contingent work arrangements dramatically restructure the relationships between worker and organization. Before the 1970s when organizations in the United States began to downsize and restructure and rely more on contingent labor, employees often felt that they and their organizations were invested in one another for a lifetime and were strongly committed to it. As organizations have provided less job security and workers are less invested, workers have decreased their commitment and loyalty. The academy has mirrored the general labor market, with the number of non-tenure-track faculty increasing since the 1970s. In examining non-tenure-track workers in the academy, Umbach (2007) used social exchange theory to examine how the new contracts transform relationships between workers and the organizations in which they are located. According to Umbach (2007), "Social exchange theory posits that individuals form relationships with those who can provide resources. In exchange for these resources, individuals will reciprocate by providing resources and support, thus, individuals will exhibit greater commitment to an organization that they feel supported and rewarded them" (p. 93). Social exchange theory suggests that individuals under contingent work conditions would exhibit lower levels of commitment and potentially lower performance. Umbach (2007) notes that studies of contingent workers in industry and business show that they are less committed to employers and perform at lower levels than permanent workers. We question, however, whether faculty (as professionals) can be compared with laborers in terms of commitment and orientation to work. Most employees in the overall workforce do not have the long-term training and socialization that faculty have. Studies focused on freelance or contingent computer technicians, nurses, engineers, and other professionals have not found them lacking commitment; such workers are more apt comparisons for faculty (Connelly and Gallagher, 2004; Hipple and Stewart, 1996).

Other studies using the perspective of economics have looked at the way labor market principles shape the working conditions of non-tenure-track faculty. Both a supply of individuals willing to work part time and a demand from employers for part-time labor must be present. The wages and working conditions are often determined by the interaction of supply and demand. If a large supply of individuals is willing to take part-time employment, then wages and working conditions are likely to be less favorable. Economists also study whether certain groups of individuals may be more or less sensitive to wage increases. Faculty may enjoy the nature of the work to such an extent that they are willing to take lower wages to be involved in this type of work. In other cases, individuals may need more flexible work arrangements because they care for dependent children or adults and are thus willing to accept lower wages. Data suggest that non-tenure-track faculty have many different motivations: some teach for the love of being in the classroom and are retired, and others teach for a second income, but neither group depends on their salary as non-tenure-track faculty for total wages. This oversupply of individuals who are less concerned with wages and working conditions creates a situation where wages and working conditions remain low for the overall population of part-time and non-tenure-track workers. Toutkoushian and Bellas (2003) found that women are much more likely to prefer part-time employment for the flexibility it offers despite lower salaries, thus helping to create an oversupply of part-time faculty. These types of studies help to highlight the difficulty in creating more equitable conditions, as many people teach without concern for pay, while others depend on the salaries.

Another economic theory that has been brought to bear on non-tenure-track faculty is risk-taking theory. Cross and Goldenberg (2009) suggest that faculty are well aware that the statistical likelihood of a graduate student's ending up with a tenured position upon completion of a degree is extremely low. They postulate that this fact is now universally recognized and that graduate students are aware of the tight job market and the decline in tenure. They even suggest that faculty members were warned about enrolling in graduate programs and the poor prospects of jobs but that these warnings did not reduce enrollments. Cross and Goldenberg (2009) gloss over how having larger graduate programs benefits the school in other economic ways, despite knowing that fewer jobs are available for graduating students. They perceive that graduate students understand that their odds of obtaining tenure-track jobs are low but believe they are willing to take the risk because they see a positive upside. They note, "Entering graduate school is thus like entering a lottery in which a win is a tenure track position and a loss is some alternative career. Those who purchased a lottery tickets do so in hopes of winning the grand prize. For nearly everyone, that hope is not fulfilled, but for most, the loss (the cost of the tickets) is not a disaster" (Cross and Goldenberg, 2009, p. 79). They suggest that if individuals do not obtain a tenure-track job, they enter some other alternative career that is also interesting and relatively respectable or a non-tenure-track job that is similar to their original goal. They describe how graduate education has moved increasingly away from an egalitarian culture toward a more competitive culture and marketplace, with this lottery-type system for obtaining a tenure-track faculty position. Thus, they suggest that non-tenure-track faculty go into graduate school and their early faculty career knowing a tenure-track position is unlikely and that some alternative career (a non-tenure-track position or entering another field) is much more likely.

Although economic theories are a primary lens for understanding non-tenure-track faculty, available evidence does not support some of the economic theories. As demonstrated in Kezar and Sam (2010), even though non-tenure-track faculty should exhibit less commitment, studies demonstrate that they have equal or more commitment than tenure-track faculty members (Maynard, 2000). Studies about the experience and understanding of non-tenure-track faculty demonstrate that they do not have a detailed understanding of the labor market as suggested by economists and did not understand how difficult it would be to obtain a tenure-track position (Baldwin and Chronister, 2001; Schell and Stock, 2001). In fact, the number of non-tenure-track faculty has been rising rapidly, and with doctoral degrees taking five to ten years to complete, it would be almost impossible for doctoral recipients to have evaluated the situation appropriately as economic theories would suggest. In addition, as research acknowledges, faculty members do not come to academe for money and traditional economic gain and are therefore less likely to follow labor market trends than those in other fields (Schuster and Finkelstein, 2006a). So the culture of academe itself may make some economic theories and analogies less viable for understanding the behavior of faculty. This observation is not to say that economic theories are not valuable but that they have been marginally successful in understanding or explaining the behavior of non-tenure-track faculty as currently applied. We need more robust applications of economic theory that acknowledge the professional training and background of faculty. Moreover, because economic theories are so often used, we need researchers to be more critical about whether they are applicable and in what situations.

Sociological Theories

Sociological theories such as professionalization, deskilling, and academic capitalism have also been drawn upon to understand the behavior and experience of non-tenure-track faculty. Rhoades (1996) uses professionalization theory to problematize the move away from tenure to more non-tenure-track faculty positions. Although many economic theories treat faculty as laborers, Rhoades (1996) and others use professionalization theory that suggests that faculty are professionals who operate under a different set of principles and standards from other employees or laborers. As professionals, they are autonomous and not directed by managers. It is argued that professional groups seek autonomy, manage themselves, and create their working conditions because they can best establish the working conditions that will further their complex jobs (Sullivan, 2004). Two perspectives exist on professionalization. The first perspective views professionals as those who serve clients and society, therefore obtaining autonomy by living up to a higher standard or work ethic. They hold a high standard of work by implementing certain internal regulations such as peer review, self-policing, and clear professional codes of ethics and standards. Society grants professionals certain privileges such as autonomy, academic freedom, control of their work environment (governance), and tenure because professionals live up to these internal high standards, work aggressively at self-regulation, and are accountable rather than depend on external mandates (Sullivan, 2004).

Although Sullivan and others view professionals in idealized terms, the other perspective is less flattering. Rhoades (1998) critiques professionals as "maintaining monopolies of expertise" and casts professionals as "self inter-ested groups that serve the interest not of their clients and society but of them-selves" (p. 20). He notes that faculty have struggled to establish autonomy from managers and boards over the last century. In his view, the concept of professionals is connected to a political struggle with other types of workers. With this lens, professionals are not as positively value-laden; instead, they are merely asserting power and a privileged role in relationship to others. Rhoades notes that feminist studies, labor studies, environmental movements, and con-sumer movements have also voiced his concern about professional expertise. In particular, labor studies and the union literature are critical of the notion of professionals, viewing it as creating an artificial hierarchical arrangement where certain groups are privileged over others. Professionals tend to be anti-union and not see themselves as united with other workers against manage-ment (Gulli, 2009). Although Rhoades (1998) believes that traditional notions of professionalism need to be challenged insofar as they support hierarchy and self-interest, they also are perhaps not to be entirely abandoned because pro-fessionalism has other inherently good qualities such as empowering workers and more democratic work conditions.

In the various critiques of professionalization theory in recent years, schol-ars have examined the failures of professions to live up to their ideals (Hamilton and Gaff, 2009; Sullivan, 2004). Sullivan (2004) reports how faculty are sup-posed to "weed out" colleagues who do not live up to the expectations of the profession, but few faculty are actually asked to leave when they have sub-standard performance or act inappropriately. In other words, the self-policing that is part of professions has largely not occurred in academia. Even though professionals have codes of ethics, faculty socialization largely does not enforce these codes and professional standards do not play a large part in graduate edu-cation. In the public's eye, professionals have not lived up to their internal set of standards and therefore the privileges awarded such as tenure, autonomy, and control of work may no longer be tenable options (Sullivan, 2004). As Rhoades notes, "The 1970s, 1980s, and 1990s brought increased critique of and challenge to academic norms, autonomy, and job security. Faculty have been crit-icized for norms that focus more on their peers than serving undergraduate clients, more on research than teaching, and more on career self interest than on the public interests" (1998, p. 132). Rhoades also suggests that faculty are internally stratified and that this stratification does not necessarily serve the profession well. Instead, the stratification creates classes of elites who control other professionals rather than create the type of autonomy intended by professionalization. Full professors are able to exert more control, and certain groups of faculty such as those who can obtain large grants ("academic capitalists") enjoy more freedom and experience a different work life from other faculty members.

Several sociologists raise the question of whether faculty work is best suited to being considered a profession (with autonomy and professional control) or as managed labor (being managed by people with authority and held accountable externally). Although Rhoades (1996) does not address the professional misgivings of the academy, he emphasizes that the faculty position, by its very nature, thrives more when professionals control the work environment. As noted earlier, however, Rhoades does concede that professions are monopolies and are also largely self-interested. Various authors arguing for faculty to maintain their status as professionals suggest that faculty are likely better able to choose those who should enter the profession and socialize them to their positions; make decisions about teaching and learning and curriculum delivery to have control over their intellectual property; and have input into their salary, job security, and working conditions (Baldwin and Chronister, 2001; Finkelstein and Schuster, 2006b; Gappa, Austin and Trice, 2007; Hamilton and Gaff, 2009). Faculty are more likely to make better decisions related to these issues because they are closer to the ground and know how to design an environment that will work for students (Sullivan, 2004).

The decision about how to conceptualize faculty is extremely important; if it is generally agreed that faculty (whether tenure track or nontenure track; full time or part time) are professionals, then particular theories and assumptions are adopted. If scholars conceptualize non-tenure-track faculty as inherently not on a professional path, however, then economic theories may make more sense to understand their experience, contributions, and impact. One challenge to studies comparing non-tenure-track faculty with tenure-track faculty can occur when non-tenure-track faculty are conceptualized as laborers, while tenured and tenure-track faculty are conceptualized as professionals in an institution, resulting in different rights and responsibilities, as well as different expectations from others. Rhoades (1998) conceptualizes faculty (both tenure track and nontenure track) as becoming hybrids—managed professionals—increasingly moving away from a professional status and becoming laborers. Shaker's study (2008) of the full-time non-tenure-track faculty experience supports this concept; it found that non-tenure-track faculty appear to be hybrids—neither laborers or professionals, but possessing qualities of both.

Related to the notion of professionalization is the concept of "deskilling" (Rajagopal and Farr, 1992; Rajagopal, 2004). Throughout the last one hundred years, the move has been to routinize and deskill labor in bureaucratic organizations and to take away the complexity that often led to a better product for a cheaper, similar product. The role of managers is to determine ways to take parts of the skilled labor and develop automated processes to do similar or related work more cost-effectively. Various scholars suggest that the same process of deskilling is happening in the academy and that it threatens the quality of the academy and the teaching and learning environment (Rajagopal and Farr, 1992). One example is the move away from individualized syllabi to departmental or unit syllabi (or standardized lower-division courses) that can be taught by any faculty member and are not specific to the expertise of any one faculty, often with limited faculty input. Another example is the common curriculum for online courses.

Another sociological theory that has been brought to bear to understand the rise of non-tenure-track faculty is the notion of academic capitalism. Slaughter and Rhoades (2004) have examined the trend in the academy to commercialize and commodify operations, which is part of a larger global trend and tied to a neoliberal philosophy. Neoliberals assert that society is best served when public functions are privatized and market values drive political, economic, and social institutions. This general philosophy applied to higher education means a public divestment from higher education, which can be better delivered through private sources such as for-profit institutions and private colleges. For the existing public institutions, neoliberalists would recommend that market principles drive services and operations. For example, if it is less expensive to run residence halls through an external contractor, then the institution should move to outsource that function. Many people are critical of this philosophy and its effect on the academy, moving from predominantly educational values to market values that can compromise the educational mission (Slaughter and Rhoades, 2004; Kezar, 2004). The link to non-tenure-track faculty is that their employment conditions operate much more like the U.S. economic market in which companies have largely moved to a contingent workforce. Rather than seeing higher education organizations as institutions that comprise professionals and operate under a professional code, neoliberalism provides the logic for operating campuses like corporations. Various studies have shown how higher education has shifted in the last thirty years to operate more like corporations, employing cost-saving measures, using more hierarchical leadership and management, and displacing professional self-regulation with external accountability processes (Kezar, 2004).

Sociological theories point to the systemic nature of the transition from a largely tenure-track to a largely non-tenure-track faculty under neoliberal philosophy. Scholars using sociological theory argue that this change has gradually taken place over a long period of time but is deeply embedded in the United States and other worldwide economic, social, and political systems. Yet these theories reinforce the notion that current conditions are fixed and do not contest the nature or the direction toward a commodified and corporatized academy. Sociological theories also demonstrate the decline in rationale behind professionals and their stature in society. Sociological theories are often helpful for understanding why certain trends occur, but they are less helpful for understanding the experience of non-tenure-track faculty or a way forward.

Psychological and Social Psychological Theories

To understand the experience and effect of non-tenure-track faculty, many scholars have used social psychological and psychological theories. Many psychologically framed studies have come from a deficit model, suggesting that non-tenure-track faculty lack qualities that are important to a functional workplace such as commitment, satisfaction, social capital, agency, the ability to learn and form collegial relationships, and the ability to integrate students on campus. The deficit framing often masks the reality that these faculty, for example, may not be less committed than tenure-track faculty. Authors sometimes acknowledge that they take a deficit perspective because of the poor working conditions for non-tenure-track faculty (which is understandable), but this deficit assumption may not be accurate. It is important that researchers examine their assumptions carefully to more accurately discover the dynamics in play.

The issue of commitment is an important construct in psychology that is often examined in studies of employees. The move to a largely non-tenure-track faculty in which the organization provides less job security raises the question of individual commitment. Studies demonstrate that people with high levels of commitment tend to stay with organizations, resulting in less turnover, better morale, and increased function on their work (Bland and others, 2006). Although much of the commitment literature has focused on contingent employees in corporations, faculty as professionals go through extensive training for their positions and are likely to be more strongly committed than other contingent workers. So far studies of commitment have had mixed results, with some suggesting that non-tenure-track faculty have the same or higher commitment than tenure-track faculty and others suggesting they have less (reviewed in more detail later). But the current framing, drawing on theories from business focused on clerical workers and other non-professional workers, does not take into account the differences in faculty socialization and training—the professional element of faculty work.

To gain a better understanding of faculty motivation rather than viewing non-tenure-track faculty through a business lens, they could be equated with contingent professionals in other fields such as medicine. For example, organization-based career theory—a four stage model of professional careers—is used to help understand commitment levels of medical laboratory professionals (Blau, 1999) and may also be applied to non-tenure-track faculty. This theory takes into consideration the socialization processes of professionals as they enter a working community and determine commitment based on moving from the first level of apprenticeship to further levels of expertise in the community. This theory could also be used to understand the various mixed results of non-tenure-track faculty members' commitment to institutions; for example, non-tenure-track faculty who never move into full socialization in an academic community may be less committed compared with those who are included and socialized into the profession.

Studies have also examined the concept of satisfaction, although in largely atheoretical ways. Many researchers appear to come into a study to demonstrate that non-tenure-track faculty are dissatisfied (again using a deficit model), only to discover they are generally as satisfied as tenure-track faculty. An exception is Maynard and Joseph's study (2008), which investigates satisfaction as tied to the fit between a person and a position or job and whether an individual feels underemployed. Underemployment is "when an individual holds a job that is somehow inferior to or of lower quality than a particular standard" (p. 141). Underemployment has several dimensions: more education than is required for the job, involuntary employment in a field outside of one's area of education, more skills or experience than required by the job, involuntary employment in part-time or temporary work, and low pay relative to a previous job or others with similar educational backgrounds. Individuals who are underemployed are expected to be less satisfied and to have a variety of negative outcomes such as poor job attitude and job performance and adverse effects on their family and social relationships. Various empirical studies provide evidence that when job demands are aligned with a worker's abilities, the resulting fit has positive consequences (Maynard and Joseph, 2008; Bretz and Judge, 1994; Caplan, 1987).

Non-tenure-track faculty generally fit into many of these conditions of underemployment, as they receive lower pay than other colleagues for the same work and are in temporary part-time positions. Underemployment occurs, however, only when the employee desires full-time employment or higher pay. Theories of person-job fit suggest that we need to look at individual employees' preferences rather than assume that all employees have the same desired working conditions and specifications. Maynard and Joseph's study (2008) empirically demonstrates that the perception of the individual is the most important factor in determining underemployment and person-job fit, which translates into satisfaction and the way individuals experience their job. Their work extends to even the studies that have looked at differences by group, for example, the satisfaction among certain groups of non-tenure-track faculty (those who have another job or teach for pleasure rather than pay) and the dissatisfaction among non-tenure-track faculty who would prefer a tenure-track or full-time position. They demonstrate that even individuals in these groups vary based on their perception of underemployment.

Another social psychological theory—social capital—has been used to explore the impact of non-tenure-track faculty on students. Social capital theorists suggest that students can develop knowledge that will make them successful by creating networks with other important people in the educational context. The more students interact with faculty, the more likely they are to develop relationships and connections and in turn develop informal knowledge that will help them in the future. Students who interact mostly with non-tenure-track faculty may be disadvantaged because these faculty have little time to interact with students. Jaeger and Eagan's research (2009) suggests that students who are in two-year institutions or remedial education and introductory courses in four-year institutions are more likely to have non-tenure-track faculty who do not have the time to play nurturing and guiding roles, which are particularly important to students who lack access to social capital in their daily lives. Institutional agents help students to navigate the institution, to be successful in classes, and to learn all the implicit knowledge about how to be successful in the environment (Jaeger and Eagan, 2009). Social capital emphasizes both the agency and work by students but also the social environment that surrounds them and the types of accessible networks on campuses with large numbers of non-tenure-track faculty. It is hypothesized that fewer networks are available for students to tap into and that there are fewer institutional agents that can help them as non-tenure-track faculty numbers grow on campuses.

To understand the impact of non-tenure-track faculty on student outcomes, several scholars have examined theories of involvement, engagement, and student integration (Benjamin, 2002; Jacoby, 2006; Jaeger and Eagan, 2009; Eagan and Jaeger, 2009; Umbach, 2007). Benjamin (2002) and Jacoby (2006) hypothesize that the overreliance on part-time non-tenure-track faculty could undermine successful student integration and retention on campus, and Bettinger and Long's studies (2005a, 2005b) on part-time faculty suggest that they affect students' interest in subject areas and second-semester retention. Studies have demonstrated that as students become academically integrated on campus, they are more likely to be retained. A factor in academic integration is interaction with faculty members and availability of faculty for the student. Therefore, these authors hypothesize, the reliance on part-time faculty could hinder academic integration because many part-time faculty are not present on campus as often as other faculty. Umbach (2007) also posits that non-tenure-track faculty, particularly part-time faculty, may affect students' success because non-tenure-track faculty are unable to spend as much time with students. Faculty engagement with students is an important characteristic that has been found to lead to students' success. The studies are inconclusive on this issue (for example, findings that are statistically not significant, findings that lean in both directions, or methodological limitations), and the concern about whether non-tenure-track faculty affect student integration remains a hypothesis with only limited evidence in support of this hypothesis.

Another psychological theory that has been used to understand non-tenure-track faculty is psychological contact theory. As noted earlier through social exchange theory, in some studies non-tenure-track workers (in other fields) demonstrate lower commitment and performance in the organization, but findings have been mixed. As individuals with lower commitment and performance interact with other employees in more permanent work conditions, it can affect the overall morale of the organization. In addition, long-term employees may feel less secure about their job status because of the increasing number of contingent or part-time workers employed by the organization. Therefore, job performance can decline for not only non-tenure-track faculty members but also for tenured faculty members who sense that the implicit contract between employee and employer has been broken (Umbach, 2007). Yet it remains a hypothesis, and we do not have empirical proof in the academy of this phenomenon.

Hollenshead and others (2007) use Maslow's theory of human motivation to examine a host of perceived needs or concerns of non-tenure-track faculty. They suggest that their concerns fit into his framework and that this lens can help to explain their behaviors. Maslow suggested that "people require certain conditions in their lives, and that each lower level of need must be realized before a person is motivated to seek fulfillment of a higher level need" (Hollenshead and others, 2007, p. 11). Administrators perceive non-tenure-track faculty to have several basic needs: increased compensation (75 percent), job security (72 percent), respect (70 percent), and working conditions such as office space and equipment (61 percent). Interestingly, the issue of respect would not necessarily fall into Maslow's more basic needs (but are important in his second stage of belonging and self-esteem) and suggests that the issue of inclusion and valuing non-tenure-track faculty may be just as important as some of these basic needs. Administrators perceive that non-tenure-track faculty cared less about promotion (33 percent), research support (26 percent), access to the tenure track (23 percent), and governance (11 percent). Hollenshead and others (2007) point out that non-tenure-track faculty are a very diverse group, however, that some are getting their needs met in work outside the academy; moreover, administrators are likely to misunderstand many of their non-tenure-track faculty members unless they speak to them regularly because of the group's heterogeneity. They note that generalizations about needs are difficult to determine.

O'Meara, Terosky, and Neumann (2008) suggest the primary lenses for understanding faculty members are agency (the ability to assume) and learning (the ability to learn and change, personally and professionally), which lead to growth and development—the heart of understanding faculty members. They hypothesize that non-tenure-track appointments create different opportunities for learning to inform one's work. They define agency as the desire to create a work context conducive to thought over time. Agency is affected by the way faculty roles are constructed and whether they can create time to think and learn. As they note, "Appointment types and job security may change faculty access to important work resources or feelings of agency in gaining access to resources and time" (O'Meara, Terosky, and Neumann, 2008, p. 29). The authors suggest that non-tenure-track faculty are constrained in their ability to learn or have agency and are thus stripped of their access to a professional and meaningful career. They go on to also discuss professional relationships and commitments such as being an activist on campus or being involved in one's teaching as possible other sources of being a professional that non-tenure-track faculty appointments often make difficult. They suggest that until agency, learning, and the ability to form relationships and commitments are addressed, non-tenure-track faculty are fundamentally constrained from being full professionals. In our earlier research, we found much evidence to suggest that the hypothesis of O'Meara, Terosky, and Neumann (2008) about the limitations of non-tenure-track faulty to work as professionals is accurate (Kezar and Sam, 2010).

An overarching concern with psychologically based studies is that they may ignore societal and organizational conditions that shape non-tenure-track faculty behavior and outcomes. Most of the studies do not control for varying working conditions and different contexts that non-tenure-track faculty find themselves in. Also, only a limited set of work examines important differences in motivation and examines nontenure track as a heterogeneous group that is situated within very different working conditions making general explanations quite difficult.

Organizational Theory

Organizational theory has been used more tacitly than other theory bases. Studies that have examined current policy and practices related to non-tenure-track faculty often take an organizational perspective but do not cite any specific theoretical concepts or works. Organizational theory tends to focus on concepts, trends, and changes that happen at an institution or campus. Economic and sociological theories sometimes question the scope of organizational theories, as the latter ignore broader forces that brought non-tenure-track faculty into being. Rhoades (1996), for example, questions what he terms "functionalist organizational theories" that he feels take the non-tenure-track faculty situation as a given (that they now exist, so we need to create policies and practices to support them). His sociological work demonstrates how non-tenure-track positions emerged and focuses on reversing this trend rather than accepting it, which he feels functionalist apolitical studies tend to do. By stepping back from the institution and examining broader trends, we might question the move toward non-tenure-track faculty. Rather than providing policies and practices to support non-tenure-track faculty, we should focus on creating more tenured positions and strengthening the institution of tenure.

Examples of scholars who use an organizational approach are Gappa and Leslie (1993) and Baldwin and Chronister (2001). We note, however, that organizational theory has been used only tacitly, as these authors do not frame their research in any particular organizational theories and concepts. Instead, they focus their research on the organizational level and at non-tenure-track faculty as an empirical reality. At present, organizational theory has been underused. We agree with Rhoades (1996) that many studies have examined non-tenure-track faculty in the organization but have not explicitly applied specific theory to understand non-tenure-track faculty.

One theoretically informed study examined the organizational concept of productivity (Bland and others, 2006). Studies of faculty productivity find that three main characteristics (individual faculty qualities, environments, and departmental leadership) lead to more productive departments in terms of grants, articles, effective teachers, and committed faculty (Bland and others, 2006). The environmental characteristics that enhance productivity include a decentralized organization, recruitment of driven faculty, clear mission and goals, shared culture of excellence, positive group climate, sufficient size and diversity, mentoring, communication and networks, resources, adequate work time, rewards, and opportunities for professional development. Almost all of these departmental qualities are missing for non-tenure-track faculty and, as we discuss later, most likely affect their ability to be productive. Bland and others' study (2006) demonstrated how non-tenure-track faculty have less access to productivity-facilitating features of the workplace such as professional development, rewards, clear expectations, mentoring, and participation in governance. Bland and others (2006) hypothesized that the tenure system is a major organizational mechanism for ensuring the presence of the environmental features necessary for productivity. Certainly, as they claim, tenure is a system that can help to operationalize the positive features such as mentoring, communication, autonomy, and commitment, but it does not necessarily follow that other systems or approaches in place could not also meet these goals.

Labor Relations Theory

Labor relations theory has an interdisciplinary perspective and attempts to fuse economics principles, sociology of work, and political science ideas such as conflict and power. This discipline provides some insight into the way that an interdisciplinary perspective might enhance our understanding by drawing on key concepts across a host of disciplines. Because of its interdisciplinary focus, labor relations theory ranges from understanding the status quo of employee-employer dynamics and the relation of employees to work to theories of mobilization and enacting change. For example, Tilly (1996) uses institutional theory as one of his theoretical lenses to better understand the current relationship among employers and labor markets and employees. He uses institutional theory to understand how firms create various types of labor markets, depending on their needs (flexibility, cost minimization, and predictability) and constraints (physical technology, social technology, available workforce, and state policy), which results in the availability of various types of work, especially involuntary part-time work. Tilly argues that as a result of the power that firms wield, the only way workers can become active agents in the labor market is to be a collective and unionize.

Labor relations theories also focus on unions and their role in the workplace. Theories that conceptualize the relationship among unions, faculty, and administration are helpful because academic unions such as the NEA and the AFT, and even nonacademic unions such as the American Federation of Labor and Congress of Industrial Organizations, are increasingly part of the academic staffing landscape. At the other end of the labor studies spectrum, instead of studying how things are, labor relations theories can be used to understand mobilization toward change or activism—moving toward how things should be (depending on one's perspective). For example, Alinsky's work (1971) on community organizing and grassroots change incorporates the politics and economics involved in a change movement while also noting struggles for power and ways to confront the status quo. Scholars like Berry (2005) and Nelson (1997) use labor relations theories as a call to galvanize non-tenure-track faculty to some sort of activism to help change the academy. Those works that focus on unions and the relationship of unions to the academy often focus on the changing labor markets, reestablishment of faculty and administrative roles, and the need for change (Burke and Naiman, 2003).

This "call to action" component of many labor relations theories is a component not often explicitly found in the other categories of theory described in this chapter. The sociological and many of the psychological and social psychological theories applied to studying non-tenure-track faculty tend to be more normative or descriptive in nature. For example, academic capitalism explores the nature of the status quo and how it became that way and studies on satisfaction and commitment focus on the level of commitment held by non-tenure-track faculty, but few of the theories look to changing the dynamic that currently exists. Though these lenses are useful, labor relations theories help provide a counterpart. Many of the labor theories draw from different areas of the previous disciplines. These theories focus on activism, which is prescriptive in nature, finding ways to get people involved from the bottom up rather than explaining the reasons why people get involved. In our earlier work (ASHE Higher Education Report, vol. 36, No.4) regarding plans of action and recommendations, we hearken to the importance of change occurring from the bottom up rather than relying on change to happen from those higher up in the institutional hierarchy.

Conclusion

This chapter provided an overview of the most prevalent theories that have been applied to understand non-tenure-track faculty. Our review suggests that non-tenure-track faculty as a phenomenon is undertheorized and that too few theoretical lenses have been applied to understand this broad and important landscape. By "undertheorized," we mean that many studies are conducted with little attention to theory or the range of theories that might help to understand a particular research question. Also, research questions may be posed quite narrowly because of the theory brought to bear focusing on psychological issues and ignoring societal and organizational ones. And some theories (organizational theory, for example) have not been explicitly used, which prevents a fuller understanding of non-tenure-track faculty. We also believe that more interdisciplinary work (such as labor relations) might help address some of the complex questions. We believe the underlying assumptions brought to the study of non-tenure-track faculty will continue to need examination in coming years.

We explored three major assumptions: (1) whether faculty are laborers or professionals; (2) a deficit or asset model for faculty; and (3) whether contingency is the new norm for academic labor or whether it should be critiqued and not accepted as the norm. Evidence suggests that faculty are hybrids (both professionals and laborers) and that we need to embrace assumptions from both sets of literature (sociology and economics) and broaden the scope of future studies. As noted in the chapter, studies are often framed from a deficit perspective, no matter what discipline is applied. Non-tenure-track faculty are studied for what they lack, not for the assets they have or the hurdles they overcome. Although certainly they come from a disadvantaged position in the job market, this deficit framing casts a negative light on non-tenure-track faculty as a group that is potentially damaging and inaccurate. We likely need more balance in the literature between deficits and assets. Review and application of ideas from studies of other professionals such as nurses, engineers, and computer technicians can help redirect research efforts. Lastly, much of the organizational and psychological literature accepts conditions as they are— that non-tenure-track faculty are here to stay. Yet some sociological theory and labor relations literature in particular suggest that the new status quo does not need to be accepted. Unions have been pushing for change during the last twenty years but with minimal success, given the systemic nature of the changes. Labor relations literature also notes that even if non-tenure-track faculty remain part of the academic fabric, the current inequitable policies and practices are not inherent in non-tenure-track work: they can be changed.

Although these theories are appropriate to understand both part-time and full-time non-tenure-track faculty, it is likely that some concepts will play out differently for these two different groups; future research should pay attention to these meaningful differences. Part-time faculty, for example, may be closer to laborers than professionals, while full-time non-tenure-track faculty may be closer to traditional professionals than laborers. Part-time faculty usually experience more difficulty obtaining support from labor unions, and labor relations theorists need to be attentive to power differences between full- and part-time faculty.

Tensions

We can agree there *is* a problem, but not everyone agrees that it is really all that threatening.

—Thompson, 2001, p. 186

THIS CHAPTER EXPLORES the multifaceted dialogue about non-tenure-track faculty, focusing on the tensions that exist in that dialogue. An exploration of these tensions is important for several reasons. First, researchers, policymakers, faculty, and administrators tend to approach this topic with a particular ideological perspective, practical experience, and perhaps even some empirical data. The combination of limited data, ideology, and personal experience, however, leaves room for conjecture and bias, making dialogue limited and tensions more pronounced. Highlighting the research that does exist on non-tenure-track faculty may help open the dialogue to other interpretations of the data. Second, we believe that by providing several different perspectives on these various points of conflict, we might help create more productive dialogue. Juxtaposing these perspectives can inform groups of the other's perspectives. For example, the way that administrators and non-tenure-track faculty view an issue may differ quite significantly. Third, misinformation abounds about non-tenure-track faculty; by exploring these tensions, we try to dispel some stereotypes or inaccurate assumptions that have become normative beliefs that prevent productive discussion and decision making.

Determining the role of non-tenure-track faculty is a task fraught with controversy as it typically brings up the issue of tenure and its continued role in the academy. Some conceptualize the presence of non-tenure-track faculty as directly challenging the validity and worth of tenure. This chapter looks at the three kinds of tensions—ideological, practical, and empirical—that arise involving non-tenure-track faculty. We begin first with the ideological, examining how this new employment type shapes the nature of higher education and the institution of tenure. These issues are part of the broader perennial controversies surrounding the normative state of higher education: the purpose of higher education, best models to follow, and the role of the faculty and faculty work in the academy. Next, we focus on the practical tensions—everyday concerns and interests of different groups and the attainment of what is best for each group. These tensions focus on the reality that institutions experience: limited resources, conflicts of interest, and the need to compromise to try to obtain the best result. We end with the type of tension where the other two intersect: the empirical research on non-tenure-track faculty. Often the research on both non-tenure-track faculty and their impact on higher education is used to support various arguments in the ideological and practical realms. These three elements often commingle, defining the terrain where dialogue regarding non-tenure-track faculty occurs.

Ideological Tensions

When discussing part-time and full-time non-tenure track faculty and their role within the professoriate it is important to highlight the ideologies that have been used to frame the dialogue and conversation related to non-tenure-track faculty. Ideologies can privilege certain values, interpretations, priorities, and practices over others. This section examines some of the underlying ideological tensions that exist.

Conscious Creation or Accidental Development

Most scholars agree that the proliferation of non-tenure-track faculty began in the 1970s with the increase in part-time faculty at community colleges and then continued in the 1990s with the increase of full-time non-tenure-track faculty in four-year colleges and universities. The policies and practices that institutions established throughout the years have created the faculty environment with all the challenges we see today: unbalanced ratios of tenure-track to non-tenure-track faculty, bifurcated groups, inequitable treatment and compensation, and so on. Understanding the way the development occurred can play an important role in determining which path to take in our endeavors to improve higher education institutions and the faculty. Two opposing interpretations are proposed regarding the evolving situation of non-tenure-track faculty. These two interpretations can be seen as not mutually exclusive but as a gradient—at the one end the conscious creation of an exploited class of faculty and at the other the accidental development of a non-tenure-track workforce.

Scholars such as Rhoades (1998) and Berry (2005) argue that the policies and practices regarding faculty were the result of deliberate administrative choices. Slaughter and Rhoades (2004) argue that the current exploitation of non-tenure-track faculty is just one result of academic capitalism—the corporatization of higher education as it engages in the market. With the dominant incentive being to make a profit, "academic managers" (presidents, provosts, deans) established various policies and practices based on a new model of higher education: efficient service delivery. For this new model to work, managers had to limit full-time faculty control over curriculum and academic decision making. Managers restructured the professoriat and professors' role in the institutions, separating research from teaching from service (Slaughter and Rhoades, 2004). Non-tenure-track faculty became the result of unbundling, with the majority of the population fulfilling the teaching aspect. Adding to the advantages of hiring non-tenure-track faculty would be low cost, lack of professional protections, and the inability to participate in governance (Slaughter and Rhoades, 2004; Berry, 2005).

On the other end of the spectrum, Cross and Goldenberg (2009) argue that the development of the current faculty environment was mainly a result of seemingly unrelated administrative and faculty decisions and factors coming together to create the current status quo. Rather than a conscious effort to weaken faculty as a whole or to take advantage of non-tenure-track faculty, Cross and Goldenberg (2009) note that administrators actually have little direct effect on institutions' hiring practices and that departments have more control. The administration does, however, have an indirect effect by creating incentives for departments to hire non-tenure-track faculty.

Cross and Goldenberg's study (2009) found seven types of choices that the administration and departments often make that influence non-tenure-track faculty hiring practices. First, asymmetrical errors in enrollment numbers are not addressed in planning. Because enrollment is unpredictable, schools tend to err on the side of caution: the administration assumes the lowest projected number of student enrollments and hires non-tenure-track faculty to meet any gaps. Second, only a limited number of tenure-track faculty can be hired; because tenure-track faculty are a long-term investment, institutions are very careful about hiring them. Tenure-track faculty are also simply more costly than part-time or full-time non-tenure-track faculty. Third, administrators tend to be wary of new and emerging fields, so they look to staff the department temporarily. This temporary hiring results in a department predominantly functioning with only non-tenure-track faculty without infrastructure for a more permanent hiring practice. Fourth, graduate student enrollments in individual departments or schools are limited, ultimately limiting the number of teaching assistants, as graduate students often subsidize their tuition with such assistantships. Fifth, terms of agreement with graduate student unions and their institutions; Cross and Goldenberg (2009) argue that provosts and presidents make too many concessions in the bargaining process (such as salary rates, health care, or maternity leave), which also raises the cost of graduate teaching assistants. Sixth, budget reforms such as "responsibility-centered management" (in which a predominant part of the budget is the responsibility of the individual school or college) led to both decentralization and cost-cutting practices. Seventh, the preference for researchers who are considered "stars" in their field results in the necessity to hire them at a higher price, thus taking money from other tenure-track lines and hiring non-tenure-track faculty to balance out the budget. According to Cross and Goldenberg (2009), these seven types of choices created a perfect storm of non-tenure-track faculty hiring—without necessarily intending it to be the case.

Many scholars attribute the status quo of the faculty population to a mixture of both these interpretations (Baldwin and Chronister, 2001; Gappa and Leslie, 1993; Schell and Stock, 2001). It is difficult to argue that institutions of higher education currently follow the same hiring or human resource model as they did before the non-tenure-track faculty hiring boom. It is also difficult to argue that administration had enough information at hand to be able to predict the current state of the academic faculty.

Non-Tenure-Track Faculty as a Challenge or a Solution to Tenure

The role of non-tenure-track faculty in higher education is linked to the role of tenure in higher education. Often when people discuss the state of faculty in higher education, non-tenure-track faculty hires are juxtaposed with tenure-track hires, comparing one group against the other. As reflected in some of the arguments made by Rhoades and Slaughter (2002), many in academia see non-tenure-track faculty positions in conflict with the institution of tenure. Tenure has been a staple in the last seventy years of the academic community, often linked to academic freedom as well as economic security (American Association of University Professors, 1940; Chait, 2005), and some see the rise of non-tenure positions as undermining that system. The increased hiring of a non-tenure-track workforce may serve to dismantle the tenure or tenure-track workforce by the sheer overwhelming numbers of nontenure track (Kezar and Sam, 2010). If this trend continues, eventually the population of tenure-track faculty would be reduced so that tenured faculty would be rendered inconsequential in terms of representational strength.

Scholars often divide themselves among three camps on this issue. First, academics like Benjamin (2003a and 2003b) and Finkin (1996) view the increase of non-tenure-track faculty as another means of weakening or perhaps removing tenure and whittling away at faculty autonomy and academic freedom. Second, academics such as Amacher and Meiners (2004) see tenure as an outdated practice that needs either drastic restructuring or complete removal (making everyone nontenure track to some extent). Last, academics such as Chait and Trower (1997) and Gappa, Austin, and Trice (2007) explore a middle ground or alternatives that retain many elements of tenure but are more equitable for non-tenure-track faculty.

The hiring of more non-tenure-track faculty at the cost of tenure-track faculty can be perceived as an attack on the professoriate itself. Burgan (2006) argues that tenure is not simply a mechanism to ensure job security and protect academic freedom. Rather, it is part of the larger picture of the professoriate: the role of faculty in the university as active participants in governance, experts in their field, and professional employees; and that it is symbolic of the public trust in the credibility of higher education. She contends that "the status of the professoriate as a source of public trust has been far less damaged by frontal attacks on tenure than by the growth of non-tenure-track and part-time faculty in the past two decades" (p. 170). Not only does the tenure-line faculty population become such a small majority as to be ineffectual in institutions, but also the prolific hiring of non-tenure-track faculty represents a change in mind-set regarding all faculty: disposable, outsourced, deprofessionalized, and lacking the protections of academic freedom (Burgan, 2006; Slaughter and Rhoades, 2004). To strengthen the institution of tenure, Benjamin (2003a and 2003b) suggests a reduction in non-tenure-track faculty hires, and instead institutions should move toward various lines of tenure such as a teaching tenure track to increase the value of the teaching aspect of faculty work.

On the other end of the spectrum are various advocates who view non-tenure-track faculty as the future model for the professoriate, linked with the removal of tenure or a drastically restructured version so as not to resemble what is commonly understood to be tenure (Amacher and Meiners, 2004). Amacher and Meiners (2004) argue that the current tenure structure is a flawed and out-dated model that may actually hinder quality education for students. They note the lack of accountability for instruction and a lack of innovation. Having a non-tenure-track faculty model would not necessarily endanger academic freedom or even economic security if done well. Chait and Trower (1997) conducted a study looking at two types of institutions: those with no tenure policy at all and those that are "hybrids"—schools that offer a choice between tenure and non-tenure-track positions. One of the study's findings was that academic freedom and economic security could be provided in term contracts but that, unlike tenure contracts that protect through policies and procedures, term contracts depended on "a mix of procedural safeguards, policy statements, and tradition, trust and goodwill" (Chait and Trower, 1997, p. 24). Mallon's study (2001) of schools without tenure corroborates this finding, although it found that employment issues (notice dates and dismissal procedures, promotion procedures, and faculty evaluations) tend to deviate from the policies recommended by the AAUP. To remove tenure would also be to remove the bifurcated faculty system, which, many non-tenure-track faculty note, plays a large role in the continuing disparities of treatment (Schell and Stock, 2001). There would be no hierarchy between tenured and non-tenure-track faculty.

Of course, residing in the space between the dichotomous opposites are those who acknowledge that non-tenure-track faculty hires will not necessarily decrease any time soon but they still wish to keep the institution of tenure. They look for ways to incorporate non-tenure-track faculty more into the institution and strengthen faculty as a whole (Brand, 2002; Baldwin and Chronister, 2001; Chait and Trower, 1997; Gappa and Leslie, 1993). In a case study of Indiana University, Brand (2002) acknowledged the difficulty of increasing the number of tenured faculty to meet teaching demands and suggested a move toward the conversion of part-time positions to full-time non-tenure-track faculty with established protections for academic freedom and job security. The hybrid institutions described in Chait and Trower's study (1997) would be a good example of this option. These hybrid institutions use the same requirements to evaluate faculty, offer incentives that make both the tenure track and nontenure track attractive, and give the faculty the freedom to choose either track based on his or her personal preference. At one of the hybrid schools, Chait and Trower (1997) note, the choices do not necessarily need to be permanent, for faculty have some flexibility to change tracks during a career. With these ideas, non-tenure-track faculty are seen not as a threat but as a reality and a possible new alternative to work with tenured and tenure-track faculty.

Practical Tensions

Though concerns regarding the future directions and goals of higher education help shape policies and practices for non-tenure-track faculty, ultimately there are also practical concerns that have a large impact. Limited resources of all types—monetary, facility, human—means that the needs of some may conflict with the needs of others. This section explores some of those practical tensions and the groups that are trying to navigate them.

Divisions and Tensions Among Faculty

On many campuses, faculty are often divided between tenure track and non-tenure track and at times divided further between full time and part time, leading to what some call the stratification of the university (Schuster, 2003; Thompson, 2003). Moreover, faculty members, especially non-tenure-track faculty, vary greatly in terms of workload, motivations, and responsibilities; creating subgroups within groups. These divisions can occur in informal and formal ways. For example, faculty may find themselves choosing to collaborate or socialize with some faculty members and not with others, selecting faculty members who are most similar to themselves in terms of academic experience and limiting their daily interactions with other faculty. Because of work hours or office arrangements, tenure-track faculty may have more limited contact with part-time faculty. Other divisions may be more formal based on school policies making different groups of faculty in terms of benefits, salary, and role expectations. Or separate contracts may exist for each group in unions, which means they bargain separately and may even compete for benefits.

For unionized schools, state labor laws could also directly or indirectly establish one of the formal divisions among faculty. In states such as California and New York, "wall-to-wall" bargaining units are allowed by state law (Saltzman, 2000). These units can include anyone who teaches full time or part time and in some cases may even include nonprofessional support staff, though it is rare (Saltzman, 1998). Some states such as New Hampshire and Vermont, however, keep part-time faculty and full-time faculty in separate bargaining units. The labor board of Vermont combined full-time and part-time faculty into one unit, but later the Vermont Supreme Court overturned the ruling (Saltzman, 1998). In those states that do not have this restriction, some units choose to remain separate; Southern Illinois University, for example, originally incorporated full-time and part-time faculty but eventually sought only full-timers to secure the needed signatures which was 30 percent of the proposed unit. They chose only full-timers because a wall-to-wall unit (one that includes part-time and full-time faculty) would have required a greater number of signatures to meet that 30 percent (Saltzman, 2000).

This division of faculty groups at times can give rise to conflicts of interest and tensions on campus, especially around policies and practices of resource allocation. Though not often described in this manner, the allocation in schools and departments in higher education institutions is the equivalent of a "zero-sum" game where groups have diametrically opposed interests—in this case, the limited amount of resources such as office space, class offerings, professional development opportunities, faculty positions, and benefits. Often conflict between groups can be reduced to issues around revenue and funding (Haeger, 1998). If one group receives more resources, often it means that the other groups receive less. A common critique regarding the treatment of part-time professors is the lack of office space (Gappa and Leslie, 1993; Baldwin and Chronister, 2001). If office space is limited, however, offices go more often to those faculty members assumed to be at the institution for longer periods of time: tenure-track or full-time faculty. The competing interests between groups can have a negative impact on the ability of groups to work together.

Though faculty groups may have competing interests, they also can have different needs and interests from each other—what may be of key importance to one sector may not even be a concern for the other sector. The lack of mutual interests can result in faculty groups with visions and goals that do not align with those of other groups. For example, Townsend (2003) explores the disparity between full-time and part-time non-tenure-track faculty, with full-time faculty receiving significantly more benefits and support from departments. In such a case, full-time faculty may be more interested in issues of governance, promotion, and research support (Gappa, 1996), while part-time faculty may focus more on bread-and-butter issues of equitable pay and benefits (Gappa and Leslie, 1993). Even among the part-time faculty, needs and interests may be diverse as a result of different experiences and motivations. For example, those who cobble together part-time positions for a living may have different interests from those who already have other full-time employment elsewhere. In addition to differing interests making it hard to work together, the varying interests make it problematic to come up with consensus solutions to problems on campus (such as the best ways to create professional development for faculty), as each group sees the issue from its own perspective.

Unions and Non-Tenure-Track Faculty

These practical concerns of different groups of faculty also become a concern for the unions that represent non-tenure-track faculty groups. The creation of separate bargaining units, as mentioned in the previous section, is not the only tension related to unions. Unions have dealt with their own sources of tension regarding non-tenure-track faculty. First, they encountered ideological tensions (such as seeing non-tenure-track faculty as a threat to academe). Once they began representing non-tenure-track faculty, they began to deal with practical needs and concerns. In the past, not all unions were committed to non-tenure-track faculty and were unwilling to help them bargain for rights (Schneirov, 2003). In the last fifteen years, however, non-tenure-track faculty and graduate employees have made a strong push toward organizing, and the unions have become more open to representing them. At first, it began with full-time non-tenure-track faculty, but as part-time faculty and graduate students began to increase in number, the unions have changed to reflect the new population (Dobbie and Robinson, 2008). The three unions and professional groups with the strongest influence on faculty policy (the AAUP, the NEA, and the AFT) have all taken slightly different approaches regarding non-tenure-track faculty. Though none of the unions would be considered diametrically opposed to the others, each group does seem to focus on different elements.

The AAUP's first position on non-tenure-track faculty appeared in 1987 (*Senior Appointments with Reduced Loads*), a statement that predominantly dealt with already tenured or tenure-track faculty who wanted to change to a part-time position (Gappa and Leslie, 1993). Their more definitive statement came later in 2003, *Contingent Appointments and the Academic Profession*. The statement acknowledges the growing number of non-tenure-track faculty, both full time and part time. The statement acknowledges the unfair working conditions for most non-tenure-track faculty and provides recommendations, reiterated by numerous other groups and researchers. The statement, however, reaffirms the AAUP's stance on the importance of tenure and how the current status quo on non-tenure-track faculty undermines higher education: "The dramatic increase in the number and proportion of non-tenure-track faculty in the last ten years has created systemic problems for higher education" (AAUP, 2003), listing diminished student learning, weakened faculty governance, a less-than-collegial atmosphere, deprofessionalization of faculty work, and weakened academic freedom (AAUP, 2003). The statement also goes on to say that non-tenure-track faculty in the institution should be responsible for "no more than 15 percent of the total instruction within an institution, and no more than 25 percent of the total instruction within any department" (AAUP, 2003). The AAUP is very clear, however, on the importance of shared governance and the inclusion of non-tenure-track faculty in the process. The policy statement offered by the AAUP reflects the preference for universities to strengthen tenure.

The NEA also became involved with non-tenure-track faculty. In 1988 it issued its first publication, *Report and Recommendations on Part-Time, Temporary, and Non-Tenure-Track Appointments*, emphasizing better conditions for non-tenure-track faculty and leaning toward more wall-to-wall units (Gappa and Leslie, 1993). At that time, the NEA lacked any proactive plans of action. In 2002, it released a statement regarding non-tenure-track faculty, though limiting it to only part-time and temporary faculty. Much like the AAUP statement, the NEA statement again acknowledges the poor treatment of part-time faculty and provides recommendations. It does warn that with part-time faculty, "Where part-time faculty wish to bargain collectively, they should be able to do so. However, care should be taken in determining how they will be organized and what their relationship will be with full-time faculty who might also be in a bargaining unit" (National Education Association, 2002). It continues to let locals determine whether the unit should be wall-to-wall or separate. Regarding the issue of governance, the NEA states that "the question of the role of part-time and temporary faculty in institutional governance is a thorny one" (National Education Association, 2002) and only lists the possible pros and cons of involvement. Unlike the AAUP statement, a distinction exists between full-time and part-time non-tenure-track faculty, with a preference toward full-time faculty, though several AAUP bargaining units have represented wall-to-wall faculty as well as stand-alone part-time faculty units. The NEA, however, working in conjunction with Contingent Academic Workers (CAW) did arrive at an action plan regarding non-tenure-track faculty, both full time and part time: NBI 2004-60 Action Plan. This plan incorporates elements of research (to create and update instruments and obtain accurate data on non-tenure-track faculty); organization (to mobilize non-tenure-track faculty, inform leaders, and establish networks); collective bargaining (to obtain job security, wages, and benefits through contract negotiations); political advocacy (to bring the issue of non-tenure-track faculty to a national level, including legislation and the media); leadership and capacity building (to identify and empower potential leaders and establish infrastructure for change); and communication (to provide access and ways to facilitate more dialogue regarding non-tenure-track faculty; National Education Association and Contingent Academic Workers, 2004).

In 1998 the AFT released *The Vanishing Professor*, noting the erosion of tenure-track faculty and the exploitation of part-time faculty, and in 2002 published a follow-up report, *Marching Towards Equity: Curbing the Exploitation and Overuse of Part-time and Non-Tenured Faculty*. In 2008 the AFT passed a resolution to launch a nationwide campaign called "Faculty and College Excellence" (FACE) in hopes of changing the current faculty landscape. The campaign focuses on three recommendations (American Federation of Teachers, 2008):

- To phase in prorated pay for non-tenure-track faculty;
- To have 75 percent of undergraduate classes be taught by full-time tenure or tenure-track faculty; and
- To help find ways to increase full-time tenure-track hirings while not causing job loss to non-tenure-track faculty and giving non-tenure-track faculty preferential consideration in hiring full-time positions.

The AFT does distinguish between part-time and full-time non-tenure-track faculty, as seen in separate documents for best practices. Though both encourage faculty participation in governance, historically it appears that the AFT focused more on part-time faculty than full-time non-tenure-track faculty. Again, the AFT does still hold to the traditional tenured faculty model of higher education, finding it still to be a "building block" of academic excellence (American Federation of Teachers, 2003). The AFT does, however, take a slightly different approach in wanting to convert non-tenure-track positions to tenured. It notes that "quality instruction begins with education professionals who are respected and whose work is supported by the administrators of the college or university" (American Federation of Teachers, 2008). Similar to the other groups, it stresses that an equitable environment fosters better faculty, which in turn fosters a better instructional environment and learning.

Of course, the union presence on a college or university campus alone is cause for controversy, there are both proponents and opponents to academic unions in higher education (Krause, Nolan, Palm, and Ross, 2008; Nolan, 2008; Berry, 2005; Tirelli, 1997). Advocates of non-tenure-track unions argue that it is one of the more effective ways to mobilize non-tenure-track faculty and make an impact (Berry, 2005), negotiate for equitable contracts (Maitland and Rhoades, 2005; Rhoades and Maitland, 2008), establish fair representation (Saltzman, 2000), and strengthen the faculty (Krause, Nolan, Palm, and Ross, 2008; Maitland and Rhoades, 2005). Opponents of unions argue that unions do not have the interest of non-tenure-track faculty as a main goal (Schneirov, 2003), and cause further divisiveness among faculty (DeCew, 2003). Also, as noted earlier, union representation can be perceived as a move away from professionalization and professional communities towards laborer status. Some states like Alabama, North Carolina, Texas, and Virginia have laws banning collective bargaining for all faculty (Saltzman, 1998).

Whether or not unions actually increase the use of non-tenure-track faculty is another controversy that needs further study to better understand the relationship of unionization and faculty work. In a study of unions and faculty hiring in the United States and Canada, Dobbie and Robinson (2008) found evidence to support two hypotheses on hiring. The first is that a negative correlation existed between union density and non-tenure-track faculty—higher union density meant lower non-tenure-track hiring—when the non-tenure-track unions were established early and were powerful enough to garner strong contract language and policies for non-tenure-track faculty. A positive correlation between unions and the hiring of part-time non-tenure-track faculty existed, however, when part-time faculty were not unionized early (but full-time non-tenure-track faculty were) and when the unions were strong enough to increase the difference between full-time and part-time non-tenure-track faculty (Dobbie and Robinson, 2008). The researchers themselves note that further research needs to be done on this topic to determine what the nature of the relationships are and what the relationships signify (Dobbie and Robinson, 2008).

Empirical Tensions

Up to this point, this chapter has explored the tensions regarding non-tenure-track faculty and the ideologies and practical concerns surrounding their role in the institution. This section focuses more on the tensions that arise from the empirical research specifically on non-tenure-track faculty quality, professionalism, and effectiveness (see ASHE Higher Education Report, vol. 36, No. 4, for more on the empirical research of non-tenure-track faculty). This section is particularly important, given that assertions made regarding non-tenure-track faculty often have little empirical evidence to support such claims. Many of the tensions highlighted previously in this chapter often implicitly contain assertions about the quality of professionalism and effectiveness of non-tenure-track faculty. Some view non-tenure-track faculty as a positive addition to the university (Gappa, Austin, and Trice, 2007; Gappa and Leslie, 1993; Cross and Goldenberg, 2009). Often perceptions of non-tenure-track faculty depend on the answers to surveys and interviews (Gappa, Austin, and Trice, 2007; Baldwin and Chronister, 2001; Gappa and Leslie, 1993). Hollenshead and others (2007) found that many administrators held positive views regarding non-tenure-track faculty.

Perhaps even more prolific, however, are those who see non-tenure-track faculty in a negative light, undermining the goals of higher education (Benjamin, 2002; Rhoades, 1998). In many arguments against non-tenure-track faculty, issues regarding quality and the effect on student learning have been a main focus point. The concerns about faculty quality, especially part-time faculty, may stem from a 1982 study by Leslie, Kellams, and Gunne: "Our own data suggest wide variation in the quality of instruction as provided by part-timers; at the very least we can probably generalize to the extent of saying that the quality of instruction by part-timers is less dependable. It may be superior or it may be unacceptable, but one has less assurance in advance as to which direction the variation will take" (p. 16).

Gappa and Leslie (1993) also addressed the negative assumptions that existed throughout the 1980s in various policy statements about the impact of part-time faculty on quality. The same critiques have reemerged twenty years later, and it is important that data once again be brought to bear on important questions about the impact of the increasing number of non-tenure-track faculty in the academy. Gappa and Leslie (1993) noted how many different groups, ranging from national commissions such as Involvement in Learning, policy organizations like the Education Commission of the States, and unions, all had made statements that reflected a negative assessment of part-time faculty, even though data did not exist to support these assumptions or stereotypes. Although some studies suggest that non-tenure-track faculty are less motivated and less productive (Bland and others, 2006), Shaker (2008) found full-time non-tenure-track faculty to be the exact opposite: they were highly motivated (satisfaction was intrinsic rather than extrinsic based on contract), highly productive at teaching and service (more so than their tenure-track colleagues), and generally had positive morale (although they came from campuses that had fairly good conditions for non-tenure-track faculty). These findings suggest that some of the negative effects of non-tenure-track faculty may be overemphasized in the literature or based on sparse data. Gappa and Leslie (1993) pronounced that it was time to actually look at data about part-time faculty to address these perceived negative assessments of their performance and impact on the economy. We return to this call for examination of data in the research synthesis below, looking at the elements used to indicate the quality of non-tenure-track faculty.

Faculty Quality

As with the controversies found in K–12 literature, defining "quality" faculty and instruction can be difficult (for examples, see Rothstein, 2008; Darling-Hammond, 1999; Rowan, 2000). Researchers do not agree on a single measurement to determine quality, making comparison among studies difficult as they often measure quite different aspects (Worthen and Berry, 2002). In a case study regarding a teacher accused on negligence, Worthen and Berry (2002) found that what faculty defined as quality differed from what administration defined as quality. In the following studies, quality is defined through various measures: grade distribution, student course evaluations, degrees held, contact hours and commitment, instructional styles and productivity, and students' transfer and graduation rates. These studies often provide the evidentiary support for various ideological and theoretical arguments regarding non-tenure-track faculty and may be a large basis for many preconceived notions about the quality of non-tenure-track faculty.

Grade distribution and evaluation. Both grade distribution and evaluation can be student-related indicators of faculty quality. If a faculty member tends towards grade inflation—skewing the median grades to the upper scores—it could indicate that the instructor is either not evaluating work well or not putting in the effort to make the class challenging enough for the students. In a study of grade distribution in 361 courses taught by full-time and part-time faculty at Boise State Institution, Landrum (2009) found that though part-time faculty had a slightly higher grade point average for the courses, the difference was not statistically significant (although the study did not mention whether or not full-time faculty were tenured). Landrum (2009) also found that differences in the items on the teaching evaluations were statistically insignificant. What makes both findings important, however, is that though results showed no significant differences, adjunct faculty had fewer resources available than full-time faculty. In a study looking at the grading patterns of faculty in the humanities in a community college, McArthur (1999) found that part-time faculty tended to give higher grades than full-time faculty. This result may be discipline specific, but he argues that it may make sense because part-time employment often depends on student evaluations, so there may be an incentive to make classes less difficult. In a study of student evaluations, however, Hellman (1998) noted that students' evaluations of full-time and part-time faculty differed little. At present, findings are mixed and inconclusive.

Degrees. Administration tends to be less rigorous about degree requirements for non-tenure-track faculty. Some may argue that the degrees obtained by the instructor indicate the quality of that particular instructor as a result of years of education and training (Benjamin, 2003b). Using data from the National Center for Education Statistics (NCES), Benjamin (2003b) found that most non-tenure-track faculty, both full time and part time, have fewer doctorates or first professional degrees. Though this fact may be true, the conclusion inferred from his study is that a doctorate necessarily makes a person a better instructor. He argues that the rigor of doctoral programs and experience in master's programs "provide opportunities for observing advanced instruction and engaging in instruction as a graduate assistant," (p. 81), therefore making them more qualified instructors. No empirical evidence supports this argument, however. With the argued "overproduction" of doctorates, the rise of postdoctoral positions in institutions (Ma and Stephan, 2006), the decrease in new tenure-track hirings (Schuster & Finkelstein, 2006) and the reevaluation of different academic paths (Gappa, Austin, and Trice, 2007; Bataille and Brown, 2006), we may see an increase of non-tenure-track faculty with doctorates in the future.

Contact hours and commitment to teaching. Part-time non-tenure-track faculty appear to have fewer contact hours with students, and the data about commitment are mixed. Again using NCES data, Benjamin (2002, 2003b) found that non-tenure-track faculty, especially part-time faculty, devote fewer total contact hours (instructional, informal, and scheduled office hours) than tenure-track faculty. Benjamin (2002) used these data to argue that student engagement suffers with the use of non-tenure-track faculty. Various factors may shape this interpretation, however. First, the data say nothing about the quality of the interactions or even the specific type of classroom interaction (seminar, large lecture, online, for example). Second, conclusions arrived at are uneven. Tenured and full-time faculty may hold more office hours than part-time faculty, but it does not necessarily follow that one group of students will use that time more than another. Part-time faculty often teach lower division and remediation classes more so than full-time or tenure track faculty, resulting in a different group of students. His arguments focus on non-tenure-track faculty's being unqualified for instruction rather than non-tenure-track faculty's working conditions affecting the quality of instruction they offer.

Commitment to teaching and students is often a point mentioned in discussions of non-tenure-track faculty. Benjamin (2003a and 2003b) argues that the temporary nature of the employment, lack of office hours, and numerous appointments at different institutions indicate that non-tenure-track faculty (though part time more than full time) lack commitment to teaching and students compared with tenured faculty. Umbach's study (2008) supports this argument, using the time spent preparing for class, advising, and workshop participation as variables to determine faculty commitment. He found that part timers were significantly less committed to teaching based on those variables. He does note, however, that though his study found these results, it does not necessarily mean that the fault is entirely the faculty. He argues that part-time faculty, as a result of poor treatment and resources, no longer feel committed to the institution (Umbach, 2008). The variables for a teacher's commitment, however, are directly related to the work environment; thus, full-time faculty may score higher on variables such as contact time with students because they are offered compensation and support to fulfill those tasks but part-time faculty are not. A national survey of community college faculty (both part time and full time) measuring "commitment to calling" found that groups did not differ significantly: part-timer faculty were just as committed to teaching (Freeland, 1998).

Using a slightly different measurement of commitment, Bland and others (2006) looked at the differences between full-time non-tenure-track and tenure-track faculty at doctoral institutions. Rather than measuring psychological commitment to the institutions, Bland and others (2006) defined commitment as time spent at an institution. They found that tenure-track faculty showed more commitment based on the likelihood of choosing an academic career again and the likelihood of leaving in the next three years. Commitment was higher for tenured faculty after controlling for other variables such as training and focus. This result is not entirely surprising, as the act of tenure explicitly acknowledges a long-term commitment between the institution and the faculty member that does not exist with nontenured faculty. With regard to commitment levels of non-tenure-track faculty and their institutions in terms of turnover, Hollenshead and others (2007) indicate that commitment levels among full-time and part-time faculty are similar, ranging from five to seven years at the same institution. When studying commitment to the institution, it is important to note that no studies compare tenure-track faculty who actually do not get tenure with non-tenure-track faculty. Those who have tenure are held to the gold standard of institutional commitment, while non-tenure-track faculty are the ones found lacking commitment. No mention is made, however, of the commitment of tenure-track faculty who leave the institution because they did not get tenure compared with nontenured faculty who stay with the institution despite the fact they will never be tenured.

Instructional styles and productivity. Quality is also associated with instructional styles because it is assumed that those instructors who use teaching approaches noted in key sources such as the good principles for undergraduate teaching (i.e., active learning, high expectations for students, learner centered approaches) are better than those who do not use these practices. The results are varied with regard to use of teaching styles. In community colleges, the question focuses on the difference in teaching quality between full- and part-time faculty, and the results of thirty years of studies are mixed (Outcalt, 2002). Freeland (1998) found that part-time faculty have higher expectations of their students. Digranes and Digranes (1995) found that part-time faculty tended not to use innovative teaching styles, relying more on lectures and traditional exams. Grubb (1999) did not note a difference in instructional styles, instead finding that most faculty overall often use similar traditional pedagogy. Schuetz (2002) found that part-time faculty and full-time faculty in community colleges averaged approximately the same amount of instructional time for lectures, quizzes, discussion, and exams, which Outcalt's findings on instructional time (2002) corroborate as well. She found, however, that part-time faculty were less likely than full-time faculty to update syllabi, incorporate multimedia into their instruction, and be unaware if students were taking advantage of tutoring or other academic services on campus (Schuetz, 2002). In a study of part-time and full-time instructors (no mention of whether they were tenure track or not) at different institutional levels, Umbach (2008) found that part-time faculty "place less of an emphasis on active learning, preparing well-rounded citizens, and diversity experiences" (p. 9). It is important to note that all the variables used to determine quality instruction vary depending on the researcher and the constructs created to define quality. Moreover, the use of "innovative teaching styles" or "traditional pedagogy" such as lecturing and discussion does not necessarily mean that one instructor is better than another. These studies measure the types of instructional tools used but not necessarily the skill with which they are used. Also, some of the issues examined have not been associated with quality teaching such as use of technology or updating of syllabus.

Related to instructional styles are students' interest in either the class or the major. In a study of four-year public institutions, Bettinger and Long (2010) found that students who had a part-time faculty member in their initial class tended to take 9.2 additional credit hours in that subject, compared with those students who had full-time instructors. This correlation occurred only with those part-time faculty members who were closely tied to the profession; however, although positive, the results were statistically insignificant (Bettinger and Long, 2010, 2005b). In academic subjects such as the humanities or liberal arts, those students who had a part-time faculty member took markedly fewer credit hours than those students with full-time professors.

Productivity is linked with instructional styles in this section because some have argued that those scholars who are engaged in research can bring more to their teaching than those faculty members who are not involved in research (Benjamin, 2002, 2003a, 2003b). Because of the institution's structure and goals, productivity in terms of research is not necessarily an issue at community colleges. Though faculty are not discouraged from conducting research, it is not as heavily weighted for full-time status or tenure (Outcalt, 2002). In doctoral institutions, however, productivity does play a large role. Bland and others (2006) found that tenure-track faculty are more productive in terms of research. Though Bland and others controlled for many factors: institution type, degrees, responsibilities, differences of resources for non-tenured faculty such as sabbaticals, smaller classes to teach, or even administrative support staff can weigh results in favor of tenure-track faculty.

Retention, transfer, and graduation rates. Successful completion of coursework is often an indicator of success later in life. Community college students have two options: transfer to a four-year institution or graduation. Several studies have identified a link between the number of non-tenure-track faculty at an institution or the percentage of courses students take with non-tenure-track faculty and lower retention, transfer, and graduation rates. Bettinger and Long (2005a) found that at public four-year institutions, students who have part-time faculty teach a majority of their first-year classes were less likely to return their second year. With regard to transfers, Eagan and Jaeger (2009) found, in a study of California community colleges taking place over five years, that exposure to part-time faculty affected the likelihood of a student's transferring to a four-year institution. They note that for every 10 percent increase of exposure to part-time faculty, a 2 percent decrease occurred in chances of transfer. In a follow-up study, Jaeger and Eagan (2009) found that exposure to part-time faculty affected completion of the associate degree. For every 10 percent increase in exposure to part-time faculty, a 1 percent decrease occurred in the likelihood of earning the degree (Jaeger and Eagan, 2009). Compared with the other variables in the model (part-time versus full-time enrollment, financial aid, first year GPA), all had statistically more significant effects than part-time exposure. Jacoby (2006) further explored this outcome in the graduation rates of students in community colleges on a larger scale. He found that as the part-time faculty ratio increased, the graduation rate (based on the Integrated Postsecondary Education Data System) decreased.

Ehrenberg and Zhang's econometric study of graduation rates and types of faculty at four-year institutions (2005) found that, holding factors constant, an increase in non-tenure-track faculty (either part time or full time) resulted in a reduction of graduation rates. The greatest magnitude occurred at public institutions and even intensified at master's-level institutions. Both researchers acknowledge that other reasons may account for the drop in graduation rates but do not offer alternatives.

Yet the evidence is somewhat mixed. A study comparing Texas public two-year colleges with tenure systems and those without tenure systems found no statistically significant difference in enrollment growth, affordability, and retention (Hooten, Richey, Davis, and Waller, 2009). The study did find, however, that the graduation rate was significantly higher in those colleges without tenure systems. Those institutions without tenure systems are currently the closest example of measuring non-tenure-track faculty outcomes, controlling for work environment.

Some Considerations for Empirical Research

These studies often show some differences between non-tenure-track and tenure-track faculty on issues of quality, professionalism, and effectiveness. Several concerns exist with the design, interpretation, and conclusions drawn. A challenge with many of these studies is that most of them look to outcomes and effects, but very few can adequately explain why the results are what they are. The common conclusion is often that exposure to non-tenure-track faculty produces undesirable results, so the question remains: Why do these results occur? Could other factors such as working environment be the reason that researchers see this phenomenon? Moreover, they often have not distinguished between part-time and full-time non-tenure-track faculty, which might be meaningful when it comes to hours teaching, office hours, and other areas where "part time" and "full time" may have quite different responsibilities. Even among part-time faculty, studies do not differentiate between the different types of part-timers—those who choose part-time work may have more resources available than those who are trying to create full-time work from part-time appointments.

It is important to note the distinction between the conclusion that non-tenure-track faculty are detrimental to higher education instruction and the conclusion that working conditions of non-tenure-track faculty are detrimental to higher education instruction. The first statement conflates the effects of significantly limited resources and support with the actual merit of the faculty member. The second statement acknowledges the separation of the two factors, with the understanding that until the working conditions of non-tenure-track faculty are equitable, the actual merit of non-tenure-track faculty cannot be determined. None of the empirical studies addressed in this section actually compare non-tenure-track faculty with tenure-track faculty while holding working conditions constant; however, almost all of them acknowledge the disparity of treatment and resources among the faculty (Benjamin, 2003a, 2003b; Jaeger and Eagan, 2009; Umbach, 2008; Ehrenberg and Zhang, 2005; Landrum, 2008). Very few look at differences between full-time and part-time non-tenure-track faculty in relationship to their varying working conditions, with part-time faculty having worse conditions.

The problem with the results of these studies is not necessarily the results themselves. After all, many of the findings raise important questions about the direction of higher education and possible leverage points to improve instruction for students. The conclusions drawn by researchers or other scholars, however, can be damaging—ascribing qualities to non-tenure-track faculty rather than focusing on the work environment. Though researchers clearly note the differences between working conditions and quality of non-tenure-track faculty (Jacoby, 2006), often those points are not included when others use the research to oppose the use of non-tenure-track faculty. In other professions, one would be hard pressed to argue that a person is a poor doctor, plumber, or engineer if he or she were not allotted the proper tools and environment to be able to do the work. If anything, one would lean in the direction of saying the person was a rather good doctor, plumber, or engineer if he or she did a mediocre job despite such limitations. To draw the conclusion that non-tenure-track faculty are poor faculty is not only unsubstantiated by the data but can also play a role in propagating the culture of negativity toward non-tenure-track faculty.

Numerous researchers note that a negative faculty culture and bias exist for non-tenure-track faculty, making them often feel like second-class citizens (Schell and Stock, 2001; Baldwin and Chronister, 2001; Benjamin, 2002). If tenure-track faculty are led to believe that non-tenure-track faculty are unqualified and subpar professionals and such assumptions are not challenged, it would make sense that a divisive culture would be created. This effect is magnified if the faculty have been socialized to believe that tenure-track positions are the mark of superior merit and anything less would be less ideal (Bataille and Brown, 2006; Gappa, Austin, and Trice, 2007). Full-time non-tenure-track faculty or part-time faculty might also draw the same negative conclusions. Fortunately this mind-set may be slowly changing as non-tenure-track faculty become more common and as new approaches to faculty life are encouraged (Bataille and Brown, 2006; Gappa, Austin, and Trice, 2007). Until then, however, negative assumptions are still made about non-tenure-track faculty, which in turn takes attention away from the issue of working conditions. Institutions will not spend limited resources to support faculty who are considered a second class of faculty, and tenured faculty will not support non-tenure track faculty if they feel that they are a detriment to the institution.

Other factors may also play a role in the findings of studies on non-tenure-track faculty and graduation and transfer rates. For example, non-tenure-track faculty tend to teach the bulk of remedial and introductory classes (Schell and Stock, 2001; Gappa and Leslie, 1993), which often have students who are less likely to graduate. Another explanation is that poorly resourced institutions often have to rely on non-tenure-track faculty and often serve high-risk and low-income students, who are also less likely to transfer and graduate. The research that currently exists on non-tenure-track faculty cannot determine these reasons, and further studies are necessary.

Some studies comparing and contrasting the various types of faculty sometimes compared groups that were not comparable. For example, using publications to measure the productivity of a predominantly teaching faculty may produce significantly different results from using a sample of research faculty. Care should also be taken to ensure that we do not impose expectations and measurements from tenure-track faculty onto non-tenure-track faculty when they are not relevant. For example, the benchmarks used to promote and evaluate tenured professors may not be the same benchmarks needed to understand the promotion and evaluation of a lecturer.

Conclusion

This chapter looked at the various tensions involving non-tenure-track faculty and higher education. The controversies vary from the ideological (the direction of higher education and the institution of tenure and the part non-tenure-track faculty play in those developments) to the practical (everyday concerns and interests of different groups and how to attain them) to the empirical (research on non-tenure-track faculty). In many ways these three elements intersect, creating the terrain where dialogue about non-tenure-track faculty takes place. Many leaders and change agents (whether administrators or union leaders), however, have become trapped in these various tensions as they have attempted to craft solutions. We need more open debate on the ideological tensions and brainstorming on the practical tensions.

Further research and data may help clarify some of these empirical tensions. Though large-scale data from the Integrated Postsecondary Education Data System, the National Center for Education Statistics, and the National Study of Postsecondary Faculty are useful in understanding broad trends, they lack the specificity and accuracy needed to parse differences between faculty types, institutional types, work environments, and exceptional institutions or particularly poor institutions based on the presence of non-tenure-track faculty. The other studies mentioned in this chapter often have predictive power but lack the explanatory power needed to better understand why these outcomes occur.

Conclusions and Suggestions for Further Research

PHILOSOPHICAL DISAGREEMENTS about the nature of academic positions appear to make productive recommendations difficult. In addition, poor conceptualization and deficit approaches to the study of non-tenure-track faculty have also limited our vision. And weaknesses in research designs have resulted in inconclusive findings that prevent action. We need more robust dialogue about the nature of academic appointments that moves beyond polemic arguments. We also need to have more rigorous research designs and conceptualizations. This chapter provides recommendations for addressing these challenges.

This monograph focused on research of interest to scholars of non-tenure-track faculty such as theories applied and philosophical tensions. Thus, our conclusions focus on synthesizing changes that scholars can make to the study of non-tenure-track faculty. This chapter focuses on the specifics of how non-tenure-track faculty have been conceptualized in the literature and philosophical assumptions that have affected how they have been studied. The recommendations for research emanate from a synthesis of the implications presented in the previous chapters of this monograph.

Overall Conclusions and Implications

The narrow deficit conceptualization is limiting: Researchers using only a deficit-oriented view of non-tenure-track faculty miss the opportunity for a fuller understanding of their contributions, assets, struggles, experiences, and even effects. In addition, narrowly conceptualizing the faculty as employees and not also as professionals limits a broader understanding. Although we recognize that researchers use a non-tenure-track "laborer" model that is aligned with the changing academy's more market-oriented approach, this framing does not capture the actual attitude or phenomenological experience of non-tenure-track faculty, who are generally hybrids—simultaneously professionals and employees (see Rhoades, 1998, and Shaker, 2008).

See non-tenure-track faculty as "hybrid" professionals and laborers: Studies demonstrate the commitment, intrinsic motivation, and involvement of non-tenure-track faculty; many non-tenure-track faculty view themselves as professionals with in-depth training and are socialized to the norms of the academy. Action plans created by those who work most closely with non-tenure-track faculty, including the unions, treat non-tenure-track faculty as professionals. Yet studies also demonstrate that some non-tenure-track faculty working conditions position them as laborers rather than professionals. We can advance the non-tenure-track faculty issue best by treating them as hybrid professionals and employees. But we should recognize that on some campuses they are considered professionals and on others treated more as laborers.

Address stereotypes about non-tenure-track faculty: Research demonstrates that stereotypes and misinformation related to non-tenure-track faculty abound on campuses. For change to happen in the academy, we need to address stereotypes about non-tenure-track faculty, in particular on the issues that they are of lower quality, lack commitment, move around from institution to institution, exhibit poor morale, and have other issues that are not supported by the research. Studies about non-tenure-track faculty policy changes on campuses note the importance of addressing values and beliefs about non-tenure-track faculty to avoid resistance and backlash (Kezar and Sam, 2010). These stereotypes also take an emotional toll on non-tenure-track faculty, making their already grueling jobs more difficult.

Acknowledge the heterogeneity of non-tenure-track faculty: Department, school, campus, and state policy will benefit from understanding that no single "typical" non-tenure-track faculty member exists; instead, working conditions and experiences of part-time and full-time faculty vary widely. In addition to the very meaningful differences between part-time and full-time appointments, leaders need to understand that other major differences exist: age, education, motivation, discipline, time with the institution, department, and institutional type. These differences are related to needs, concerns, contributions, experience, satisfaction, commitment of non-tenure-track faculty, and a host of other issues. When collecting data to create campus policy, these differences need to be acknowledged and explored.

Strengthen research designs: The previous chapter, "Tensions," demonstrates how researchers frame studies in ways that show non-tenure-track faculty to be of poorer quality or affect the quality of learning on campus. Many of the studies are inconclusive, find minimal differences, or do not control for important variables that might affect the results. Importantly, studies have not controlled for varying working conditions on campuses. Therefore, non-tenure-track faculty with poor working conditions are expected to perform as well as tenure-track faculty with exemplary working conditions. It is not enough for researchers to provide caveats that other issues such as larger classrooms or no compensation may account for lack of performance. Instead, studies need to be designed to control for working conditions, differences in institutional type, motivation, and discipline, for example.

Reform tenure: Although this monograph is focused on non-tenure-track faculty, all the reports, articles, and books we reviewed commented that the non-tenure-track faculty phenomenon is intimately tied to the need for reform in tenure. We reviewed philosophical nuances in "Tensions." Here we note only that as we address the issue of non-tenure-track faculty, it is important to consider reform the policies for tenure-track faculty.

Address tensions in the non-tenure-track faculty subgroups: Campuses need to be aware that non-tenure-track faculty often feel that they have competing interests and may feel tension toward each other and that it is not just the relationships between tenure-track and non-tenure-track faculty that need to be repaired. Relationships between part-time and full-time non-tenure-track faculty may need to be addressed on some campuses. Tenure hopefuls versus faculty who are happy as non-tenure-track faculty may also have a contentious relationship.

Future Research

Given that one of our observations is the inadequate knowledge we have about non-tenure-track faculty, it is not surprising that we have a list of future research areas (the first four items were presented in Kezar and Sam, 2010; the remaining four arise from this monograph): (1) the need for reliable national and state data, (2) studies that reflect the voice of non-tenure-track faculty, (3) studies based on context, (4) studies that examine differences in motivation, discipline, department, and institutional type, (5) nondeficit-based studies, (6) mixed or inconclusive results, (7) missing disciplines, and (8) interdisciplinary or multidisciplinary studies.

Reliable and Ongoing Institutional, State, and National Data

Schuster and Finkelstein (2006a, 2006b) provided one of the best overall portraits of non-tenure-track faculty using data from the National Study of Postsecondary Faculty (which is no longer available). This landscape is ever changing, and it is important that we have data that examine and categorize non-tenure-track faculty. The number of full-time non-tenure-track faculty is increasing and the number of part-timers growing; it is important that we conduct more research to understand the current portrait of non-tenure-track faculty more accurately.

Several steps could be taken to improve the data available to understand non-tenure-track faculty. First, institutions need to establish more robust systems internally to track non-tenure-track faculty, particularly differences by contract and disciplines. Given the diversity of non-tenure-track faculty and differences by institutional type, institutional data may be more helpful in creating solutions. Second, a systematic national dataset needs to be developed on all types of faculty. Perhaps UCLA's HERI faculty survey could focus more specifically on issues important to non-tenure-track faculty and explore differences in motivation, discipline, and institutional type. The recent changes to the survey are helpful, but we cannot leave the burden for this data collection on this center alone. It is important that a national database of faculty be reestablished to help inform policy, or states begin to collect data, especially if states begin to create policies related to non-tenure-track faculty.

Third, it is important to note the significance of institutional and individual participation in such data collection. To better understand the trends that are occurring in higher education, whether through national or local studies, it is imperative for institutions and individuals to participate and ensure that their voices are heard. Incentives need to be created to obtain data from non-tenure-track faculty, particularly part timers, who have not been prone to fill out phone or mail surveys.

A Voice for Non-Tenure-Track Faculty

One of the major deficits identified in empirical research is that we have little research studying the experiences and voices of non-tenure-track faculty themselves. A national database that surveys non-tenure-track faculty is no longer available. One recent national study conducted on non-tenure-track faculty examines administrators' perspectives but did not survey non-tenure-track faculty themselves (Hollenshead and others, 2007). Although we understand the working conditions of non-tenure-track faculty, we do not understand how they affect the lives of non-tenure-track faculty and how they vary among this heterogeneous group. We also understand very little about how the hostile climate on many campuses or the two-tier system affects their ability to successfully accomplish their roles. And we know very little about the psychological states of non-tenure-track faculty.

An emerging trend is for campus offices and services to survey non-tenure-track versus tenure-track faculty to determine the needs of each group so the campus can best support all faculty. Although one study compared the needs of non-tenure-track and tenure-track faculty for library use and found that they were largely the same, the situation may differ in other important areas (Wisneski, 2005). It remains an important direction for future research examining technology needs, fitness and wellness, and other support services.

Context-Based Studies

Although researchers conducting qualitative research and case studies acknowledge that institutional culture and structure affect the experiences of non-tenure-track faculty and appropriate policies and practices, most recommendations have been context free, deriving generalizations out of cases. We need more research that documents context-based solutions to address the concerns and issues of non-tenure-track faculty and studies that are formulated and framed with context as an important factor. Campus stories of change are an example of the type of context-based studies we need in the future. For example, O'Meara, Terosky, and Neumann (2008) posit that the number of non-tenure-track faculty on a campus and how long they have been there might affect their satisfaction and the perception on campus. Kezar and Sam 2010 provide examples of context based studies and recommendations that may be more helpful for institutional policy.

Differences by Motivation, Department, Discipline, and Institutional Type

Perhaps the areas most in need of research are differences by motivation, department, discipline, and institutional type. The few studies that examined motivations have found significant differences in the experiences, satisfaction, and attitude of non-tenure-track faculty. But we know less about the impact of motivation because of the limited number of studies and research that look at differences in the non-tenure-track group. Earlier researchers developed typologies of non-tenure-track faculty that encompassed motivation and background, but little research has been done using these typologies to examine differences in the experiences, outcomes, and commitment of non-tenure-track faculty. Shaker (2008) also found a set of individual differences that need to be explored in more depth—age, educational degree, career path, and time at the institution. These elements made a significant difference in faculty experiences and attitudes.

Discipline and institutional type have been investigated even less than motivation. Shaker's study (2008) is one of the few to examine a discipline—composition—in greater depth; some distinct perspectives resulted. For example, composition faculty tend to identify with their department more than the English discipline or the institution. They were cut off from tenure-track faculty and had little interaction with them. We suspect many other differences exist, for example, that salary, recruitment, hiring, and orientation differ by discipline and department. Future studies may want to further investigate this issue. Although institutional differences have not been examined in relation to satisfaction, the difference in working conditions at some institutions might also suggest some differences in satisfaction by institutional type that need to be researched in the future.

Nondeficit-Based Studies

Studies that move away from a deficit perspective can provide us a new way of understanding non-tenure-track faculty and perhaps enhance our knowledge. For example, resiliency theories to examine how people sustain themselves in difficult conditions might be helpful for understanding non-tenure-track faculty. Lave's theory (1996) on legitimate peripheral participation in communities of practice can provide insight into the faculty experience at the departmental level, especially in terms of socialization and context. Studies of resistance and critical agency might also provide insight into important organizing work currently happening nationally. Shaker (2008) provides a helpful framework for studying non-tenure-track faculty in a nondeficit perspective, using the metaphor of a scale. Studies should examine the positive features of the non-tenure-track faculty experience such as love of teaching, program environment, appreciation for academia, working with students, serving society, other non-tenure-track colleagues, and fulfillment of personal priorities. These positive features can be balanced with negative aspects such as workload, working conditions, faculty stereotypes and climate, and institutional culture while also examining specific and meaningful differences in background and experience, including age, degree, career path, time at institution, and motivation.

Mixed or Inconclusive Results

We have noted a variety of areas where studies have had varying or inconclusive results. For example, we need further study about commitment, as Maynard and Joseph (2008) conducted their study with a small sample. Their study, however, does support anecdotal reports by non-tenure-track faculty that they are highly committed. Yet Outcalt (2002) found that part-time faculty were slightly less committed. Institutional type may have an impact on the inconclusive findings, as Outcalt's study is of community colleges and part-time faculty, while Maynard and Joseph examined four-year institutions. We believe that more studies that control for or examine the heterogeneity of the faculty might also help to interpret these varying study results. In addition, we need more synthesis, as conducted for this monograph, of areas where multiple studies have sorted out the inconclusive results so more reliable information is available for policymakers and leaders.

Missing Perspectives: The Need for More Theory

Many different theories are missing from the literature, but we highlight only a few here (for example, policy and organizational theories) to suggest the need for more theorizing. Policy frameworks are mostly absent from the literature. Although many people talk about the policy implications of non-tenure-track faculty for higher education nationally, remarkably no political science theories have been brought to bear. For example, policy theories like advocacy coalition frameworks (Sabatier and Weible, 2007) or multiple streams theory (Zahariadis, 2007) look at the broader phenomenon of policy change (usually in government), but these theories can provide insight into how policies change in a smaller context such as a single university. Both these theories take into consideration context as well as attend to the individual as an agent of action. In "Theories Used to Study and Understand Non-Tenure-Track Faculty" earlier in this monograph, we noted that many studies use an organizational focus but do not use organizational theory to understand non-tenure-track faculty. Organizational fit, systems theory, organizational design, role conflict and ambiguity, need theories, organizational culture, organizational learning, power and conflict, and group polarization might all help to understand features of the experience and impact of non-tenure-track faculty.

The relationship of non-tenure-track faculty in postsecondary institutions is a complex one to understand. It involves elements of human interaction, financial and economic concerns, politics, policy, organizational structures, power and authority, culture, community, and more. Each of these elements has its own appropriate theoretical and conceptual frameworks. As we mentioned previously, the theories and conceptual frameworks that we use to understand the situation focus our attention on some factors and not on others. By expanding our theoretical and conceptual repertoire when conducting studies of non-tenure-track faculty, we may be better able to understand the role of non-tenure-track faculty and be better able to arrive at a well-informed solution.

Interdisciplinary or Multidisciplinary Studies

Our review of theories applied to the understanding of non-tenure-track faculty suggests that they tend to narrowly stem from an economic, sociological, or psychological lens. Studies would benefit from concepts and theories that use several disciplines. Interdisciplinary theories such as labor relations and political-economic theories such as deprofessionalization can also help our understanding by combining insights from various disciplines. For example, one issue that has not been well understood is the impact of non-tenure-track faculty on students' graduation rates. It appears that campuses with a higher percentage of non-tenure-track faculty have lower graduation rates. Economic, organizational, and psychological theories likely need to be combined to properly understand this issue.

So how might we address this issue? We need an economic lens to look at the types of institutions that are part of the samples and control for resources. Some may well be resources, while others are not and this can impact graduation rates not just the growth of NTTs. Further, economic theories help to understand more about the state and institutional economic conditions that might affect issues of graduation. But we also need to look simultaneously from an organizational perspective to understand variations in structure or culture that might also account for variations in graduation rates. Institutions with high concentrations of non-tenure-track faculty, for example, may have an institutional culture less committed to the teaching and learning environment, and graduation rates may be related to leadership and institutional culture rather than the number of non-tenure-track faculty. We might also use psychological theories of commitment to look at attitudes and commitment among the faculty in organizational cultures that are unstable, less committed to faculty, or resource poor. Each organizational condition might create different psychological states with different impacts on student graduation rates. Therefore, if we combine theories and frameworks, we can develop much more robust interpretations of trends that emerge in the data.

Conclusion

In the end, much work needs to be done to understand the dynamic landscape of non-tenure-track faculty. In the meantime, however, we hope to have accomplished four goals in this monograph:

To synthesize and analyze the research that is available on non-tenure-track faculty so that readers have a better understanding of these members as a heterogeneous group and their impact on higher education;

To offer different ways of conceptualizing and thinking about non-tenure-track faculty, for example, as a hybrid professional and employee;

To examine the underlying ideologies and assumptions about non-tenure-track represented in the literature and to help dispel any misconceptions; and

To help lay down the foundation for reasoned, intelligent, and ethical dialogue among stakeholders in higher education by presenting data that can be used in discussions about addressing the changes in the academy.

A very important issue has been addressed in this monograph – the need to examine our assumptions and framing of non-tenure-track faculty because it can shape whether we develop accurate research and policy.

Notes

1. We use the term *non-tenure-track faculty* because it is one of the most recognized labels for this growing class of faculty. The monograph explains, however, how campuses use a variety of different terms. We also explore the idea of using the new terminology because the term *non-tenure-track* does not recognize the professional status that we argue for in the monograph.
2. Although we have chosen not to refer to non-tenure-track faculty as *contingents* or *contingent faculty,* the workforce literature often describes workers with limited employment terms or part-time employees as "contingent"; thus, we apply the same language to nonfaculty employees.

References

Alinsky, S. (1971). *Rules for radicals*. New York: Random House.

Amacher, R. C., and Meiners, R. E. (2004). *Faulty Towers: Tenure and the structure of higher education*. Oakland, CA: Independent Institute.

Anson, C. M., and Jewell, R. (2001). Shadows of the Mountain. In E. Schell, and P. Stock, (Eds.), *Moving a mountain: Transforming the role of non-tenure-track faculty in composition studies and higher education*. Urbana, IL: National Council of Teachers in English.

American Association of University Professors (AAUP). (1940). *Statement of principles on academic freedom and tenure*. Retrieved June 1, 2010, from http://www.aaup.org/AAUP/ pubsres/ policydocs/1940statement.htm.

American Association of University Professors (AAUP). (2003). *Policy statement: Contingent appointments and the academic profession*. Washington, DC: American Association of University Professors. Retrieved February, 22, 2010, from http://www.aaup.org/AAUP/pubsres/ policydocs/contents/conting-stmt.htm.

American Council on Education (ACE). (1981). *A recent survey on tenure practices*. Washington, DC: American Council on Education.

American Federation of Teachers. (1998). *The Vanishing Professor*. Washington DC: American Federation of Teachers.

American Federation of Teachers. (2002). Marching Towards Equity: Curbing the Exploitation and Overuse of Part-time and Non-Tenured Faculty. Washington, DC: American Federation of Teachers.

American Federation of Teachers. (2003). *Full-time non-tenure track faculty report*. Washington, DC.: American Federation of Teachers.

American Federation of Teachers. (2008). AFT resolution Faculty and College Excellence Campaign. Retrieved online October, 15, 2009, from http://www.aft.org/about/ resolution_detail.cfm?articleid=1495.

American Federation of Teachers (2010). *American academic: A national survey of part-time/adjunct faculty*. Washington, DC: American Federation of Teachers.

American Federation of Teachers Higher Education. (2005). *Standards of good practice in the employment of full-time nontenure-track faculty: Professionals and colleagues.* Washington, DC: American Federation of Teachers

Association of American Universities (AAU). (2001). *Non-Tenure-Track Faculty Report.* Retrieved June 1, 2010, from http://www.aau.edu/reports/NonTenure4.01.pdf.

Anderson, E. L. (2002). *The new professoriate: Characteristics, contributions, and compensation.* Washington, DC: American Council on Education.

Baldwin, R. G., and Chronister, J. L. (2001). *Teaching without tenure.* Baltimore: Johns Hopkins University Press.

Banachowski, G. (1996). Perspectives and perceptions: The use of part-time faculty in community colleges. *Community College Review, 42*(2), 49–62.

Bataille, G. M., and Brown, B. E. (2006). *Faculty career paths: Multiple routes to academic success and satisfaction.* Westport, CT: Praeger Publishers.

Benjamin, E. (2002). How overreliance on non-tenure-track appointments diminishes faculty involvement in student learning. *Peer Review, 5*(1), 4–10.

Benjamin, E. (Ed.). (2003a). *Exploring the role of non-tenure-track instructional staff in undergraduate learning.* San Francisco: Jossey-Bass.

Benjamin, E. (2003b). Reappraisal and implications for policy and research. *New Directions in Higher Education, 123,* 79–113.

Berry, J. (2005). *Reclaiming the ivory tower: Organizing adjuncts to change higher education.* New York: Monthly Review Press.

Bettinger, E., and Long, B. (2010). Does Cheaper Mean Better? The Impact of Using Adjunct Instructors on Student Outcomes. *The Review of Economics and Statistics, 92*(3), 598–613.

Bettinger, E., and Long, B. (2005a). Do faculty serve as role models? The impact of instructor gender on female students. *American Economic Review, 95*(2), 152–157.

Bettinger, E., and Long, B. L. (2005b). Help or hinder? Adjunct professors and student outcomes. Ithaca, NY: Cornell University.

Bland, C., and others. (2006). The impact of appointment type on the productivity and commitment of full-time faculty in research and doctoral institutions. *Journal of Higher Education, 77*(1), 89–121.

Blau, G. (1999). Testing the longitudinal impact of work variables and performance appraisal satisfaction on subsequent overall job satisfaction. *Human Relations, 52,* 1099–1113.

Bowen, H. R., and Schuster, J. H. (1986). *American professors: A national resource imperiled.* New York: Oxford University Press.

Boyer, E. (1990). *Scholarship reconsidered: Priorities of the professoriate.* Trenton, NJ: Princeton University Press.

Brand, M. (2002). Full-time, non-tenure-track appointments: A case study. *Peer Review, 1*(5), 13–21.

Bretz, R. D., Jr., and Judge, T. A. (1994). Person-organization fit and the theory of work adjustment: Implications for satisfaction, tenure, and career success. *Journal of Vocational Behavior, 44,* 32–54.

Burgan, M. (2006). *What ever happened to the faculty?* Baltimore: Johns Hopkins University Press.

Burke, M., and Naiman, J. (2003). Dueling identities and faculty unions: A Canadian case study. In D. M. Herman and J. M. Schmid (Eds.), *Cogs in the classroom factory: The changing identity of academic labor* (pp. 41–57). Westport, CT: Praeger.

Caplan, R. D. (1987). Person-environment fit theory and organizations: Commensurate dimensions, time perspectives, and mechanisms. *Journal of Vocational Behavior, 31,* 248–267.

Chait, R. (2005). *Questions of tenure.* Cambridge, MA: Harvard University Press.

Chait, R., and Ford, A. T. (1982). *Beyond traditional tenure.* San Francisco: Jossey-Bass.

Chait, R., and Trower, C. (1997). *Where tenure does not reign: Colleges with contract systems (Forum on Faculty Roles and Rewards No. 3).* Washington, DC: American Association for Higher Education.

Connelly, C. E., and Gallagher, D. G. (2004). Emerging trends in contingent work research. *Journal of Management, 30,* 959–983.

Cross, J. G., and Goldenberg, E. N. (2003). How does university decision making shape the faculty? *New Directions in Higher Education, 123,* 49–59.

Cross, J. G., and Goldenberg, E. N. (2009). *Off-track profs: Nontenured teachers in higher education.* Cambridge, MA: MIT Press.

Curtis, J. W., and Jacobe, M. F. (2006). *AAUP non-tenure-track faculty index, 2006.* Washington, DC: American Association of University Professors.

Darling-Hammond, L. (1999). *Teacher quality and student achievement: A review of state policy evidence.* Seattle, WA: Center for the Study of Teaching and Policy, University of Washington.

DeCew, J. W. (2003). *Unionization in the academy: Visions and realities.* New York: Rowan & Littlefield.

Digranes, J.L.A., and Digranes, S. H. (1995). Current and proposed uses of technology for training part-time faculty. *Community College Journal of Research and Practice, 19*(2), 161–169.

Dobbie, D., and Robinson, I. (2008). Reorganizing higher education in the United States and Canada: The erosion of tenure and the unionization of non-tenure-track faculty. *Labor Studies Journal, 33*(117), 117–140.

Doeringer, P. B., and Piore, M. J. (1971). *Internal labor markets and manpower analysis.* Lexington, MA: D.C. Heath.

Dyer-Witheford, N. (2005). Cognitive capitalism and the contested campus. In G. Cox, and J. Krysa, (Eds.), *Engineering Culture: On 'The Author as (Digital) Producer.'* Brooklyn, NY: Autonomedia, pp. 71–93.

Eagan, M. K., and Jaeger, A. J. (2009). Effects of exposure to part-time faculty on community college transfer. *Research in Higher Education, 50,* 168–188.

Ehrenberg, R. G., and Zhang, L. (2004). *The changing nature of faculty employment.* Retrieved May, 12, 2009, from http//digitalcommons.ilr.cornell.edu/workingpapers/43.

Ehrenberg, R. G., and Zhang, L. (2005). Do tenured and tenure-track faculty matter? *Journal of Human Resources, 45*(3), 647–659.

Finkin, M.W. (Ed.). (1996). *The case for tenure*. Ithaca, NY: Cornell University Press.

Forrest Cataldi, F. E., Fahimi, M., and Bradburn, E. M. (2005). *2004 national study of postsecondary faculty: Report on faculty and instructional staff in fall 2003* (NCES 2005–172). Washington, DC: National Center for Education Statistics, U.S. Department of Education. Retrieved June 1, 2010, from http://nces.ed.gov/pubsearch.

Freeland, R. M. (1998). Adjunct faculty in the community college [ED 424 899].

Gappa, J. M. (1996). *Off the Tenure Track: Six Models for Full-Time Nontenurable Appointments*. AAHE Working Paper Series no. 10. Washington, D. C.: American Association for Higher Education

Gappa, J., Austin, A., and Trice, A. (2007). *Rethinking faculty work: Higher education's strategic imperative*. San Francisco: Jossey-Bass.

Gappa, J., and Leslie, D. W. (1993). *The invisible faculty: Improving the status of part-timers in higher education*. San Francisco: Jossey-Bass.

Grubb, N. W. (1999). Honored but invisible: An inside look at teaching in community colleges. New York: Routledge.

Gulli, B. (2009). Knowledge production and the superexploitation of non-tenure-track academic labor. *Workplace, 16*, 1–30.

Haeger, J. (1998). Part-time faculty, quality programs, and economic realities. *New Directions in Higher Education, 104*, 81–88.

Hamilton, N., and Gaff, J. (Eds.). (2009). *The future of the professoriate: Academic freedom, peer review, and shared governance*. Washington, DC: Association of American Colleges and Universities.

Hellman, C. M. (1998). Faculty evaluation by students: A comparison between full-time and adjunct faculty. *Journal of Applied Research in the Community College, 6*, 45–50.

Hipple, S., and Stewart, J. (1996). Earnings and benefits of contingent and noncontingent workers. *Monthly Labor Review,* 22–30.

Hollenshead, C., and others. (2007). *Making the best of both worlds: Findings from a national institution-level survey on non-tenure-track faculty*. Ann Arbor, MI: Center for the Education of Women.

Hooten, T., Richey, J., Davis, J., and Waller, R. (2009). An examination of the relationship of a tenure system to enrollment growth, affordability, retention rates, and graduate rates in Texas Public two-year colleges. *Academic Leadership, 7*(1). Retrieved February, 12, 2010, from http://www.academicleadership.org/student_research/610.shtml.

Hough, L. (2003). Higher education and its non-tenure-track faculty of the future. *Working USA, 6*(4), 12–15.

Jacoby, D. (2006). Effects of part-time faculty employment on community college graduation rates. *Journal of Higher Education, 77*(6), 1081–1102.

Jaeger, A., and Eagan, M. K. (2009). Unintended consequences: Examining the effect of part-time faculty members on associate's degree completion. *Community College Review, 36*, 167–194.

Kezar, A. J. (2004). Obtaining integrity? Reviewing and examining the charter between higher education and society. *Review of Higher Education, 27*, 429–459.

Kezar, A., and Sam, C. (2009, November). Institutionalizing equitable policies and practices for contingent faculty. Presented at a meeting of the Association for the Study of Higher Education, Vancouver, BC.

Kezar, A., and Sam, C. (2010). *Understanding the New Majority of Non-Tenure-Track Faculty in Higher Education: Demographics, Experiences, and Plans of Action.* ASHE Higher Education Report, Vol. 36, No. 4. San Francisco: Jossey-Bass.

Krause, M., Nolan, M., Palm, M., and Ross, A. (2008). *The university against itself: The NYU strike and the future of the academic workplace.* Philadelphia: Temple University Press.

Landrum, R. E. (2009). Are there instructional differences between full-time and part-time faculty? *College Teaching, 57*(1), 23–26.

Langenberg, D. N. (1998). The subfaculty. *New Directions for Higher Education, 104,* 39–44.

Lave, J. (1996). The practice of learning. In S. Chaiklin and J. Lave (Eds.), *Understanding practice: Perspectives on activity and context* (pp. 3–35). New York: Cambridge University Press.

Leslie, D. W., Kellams, S. E., and Gunne, G. M. (1982). *Part-time faculty in American higher education.* New York: Praeger.

McArthur, R. C. (1999). A comparison of grading patterns between full- and part-time humanities faculty: A preliminary study. *Community College Review, 27*(3), 65–76.

Mallon, W. T. (2001). *Tenure on trial: Case studies of change in faculty employment policies.* New York: Routledge Falmer.

Maitland, C., and Rhoades, G. (2005). Bargaining for non-tenure-track faculty. *NEA Almanac of Higher Education,* 75–83.

Maynard, D. C., and Joseph, T. A. (2008). Are all part-time faculty underemployed? The influence of faculty status preference on satisfaction and commitment. *Higher Education, 55,* 139–154.

Maynard, T. (2000). Learning to teach or learning to manage mentors? Experiences of school-based teacher training. *Mentoring & Tutoring, 8*(1), 17–30.

National Center for Education Statistics. (1997). *Instructional faculty and staff in higher education institutions: Fall 1987 and fall 1992* (NCES 97-470). Washington, DC: U.S. Department of Education.

National Education Association. (1998). *Report and Recommendations on Part-Time, Temporary, and Non-Tenure-Track Appointments.* Washington, D.C: National Education Association.

National Education Association. (2002). *NEA higher education policy statement on part-time and temporary faculty.* Washington, DC: National Education Association. Retrieved October 15, 2009, from http://www.nea.org/he/policy12.html.

National Education Association and The Contingent Academic Workers. (2004). *National Education Association and The Contingent Academic Workers: NB1 2004-60 Action Plan.* Washington DC: National Education Association.

Nelson, C. (1997). *Will teach for food: Academic labor in crisis.* Minneapolis: University of Minnesota Press.

Nolan, M. (2008). A leadership university for the twenty-first century? Corporate administration, contingent labor, and erosion of faculty rights. In M. Krause, M. Nolan,

M. Palm, and A. Ross (Eds.), *The university against itself: The NYU strike and the future of the academic workplace.* Philadelphia: Temple University Press.

O'Meara, K., Terosky, A., and Neumann, A. (2008). *Faculty careers and work lives: A professional growth perspective.* ASHE Higher Education Report, *34*(3). San Francisco: Jossey-Bass.

Outcalt, C. (2002). *A profile of the community college professoriate, 1975–2000.* New York: Routledge.

Rajagopal, I. (2004). Tenuous ties: The limited-term full-time faculty in Canadian universities. *Higher Education, 28*(1), 49–75.

Rajagopal, I., and Farr, W. D. (1992). Hidden academics: The part-time faculty in Canada. *Higher Education, 24*(3), 317–331.

Rhoades, G. (1996). Reorganizing the faculty workforce for flexibility: Part-time professional labor. *Journal of Higher Education, 67*(6), 626–658.

Rhoades, G. (1998). *Managed professionals: Unionized faculty and restructuring academic labor.* Albany: State University of New York Press.

Rhoades, G., and Maitland, C. (2008). Bargaining for full-time, non-tenure track faculty: Best practices. *NEA Almanac,* Spring, pp. 67–73.

Rhoades, G., and Slaughter, S. (2004). Academic capitalism in the new economy: Challenges and choices. *American Academic, 1*(1), 37–59.

Rothstein, J. (2008). Teacher quality in educational production: Tracking, decay, and student achievement. Working Paper No. 14442. Cambridge, MA: National Bureau of Economic Research.

Rowan, B. (2000, February). *Assessing teacher quality: Insights from school effectiveness research.* Paper presented at a meeting of the USDE Expert Panel: Strategies for Evaluating Efforts to Improve Preservice Teacher Education, Washington, DC.

Sabatier, P. A., and Weible, C. M. (2007). "The Advocacy Coalition Framework: Innovations and Clarifications." In P. A. Sabatier (Ed.), *Theories of the Policy Process.* 2nd Edition. Boulder, CO: Westview Press.

Saltzman, G. M. (1998). Legal regulation of collective bargaining in colleges and universities. *NEA Almanac of Higher Education,* 45–63.

Saltzman, G. M. (2000). Union organizing and the law: Part-time faculty and graduate teaching assistants. *NEA Almanac of Higher Education,* 43–55.

Schell, E., and Stock, P. (Eds.). (2001). *Moving a mountain: Transforming the role of non-tenure-track faculty in composition studies and higher education.* Urbana, IL: National Council of Teachers in English.

Schneirov, R. (2003). Non-tenure-track faculty: A new social movement takes shape. *Working USA, 6*(4), 38–48.

Schuetz, P. (2002). Instructional practices of part-time and full-time faculty: Community college faculty, characteristics, practices, and challenges. *New Directions for Community Colleges, 118,* 39–46.

Schuster, J. H. (2003). The faculty makeover: What does it mean for students? *New Directions for Higher Education, 123,* 15–22.

Schuster, J. H., and Finkelstein, M. J. (2006a). *The American faculty: The restructuring of academic work and careers*. Baltimore: Johns Hopkins University Press.

Schuster, J. H., and Finkelstein, M. J. (2006b). On the brink: Assessing the status of the American faculty. *Thought and Action*, 51–62.

Shaker, G. (2008). Off the track: Full-time non-tenure-track faculty experience in English. Dissertation, Indiana University.

Slaughter, S., and Rhoades, G. (2004). *Academic capitalism and the new economy: Markets, state, and higher education*. Baltimore: Johns Hopkins University Press.

Study Group on the Conditions of Excellence in Higher Education (1984). *Involvement in learning: Realizing the potential of American higher education*. Washington, DC: National Institute of Education.

Sullivan, W. (2004). *Work and integrity*. San Francisco: Jossey-Bass.

Thompson, K. (1997). Alchemy in the academy: Moving part-time faculty from piecework to parity. In C. Nelson (Ed.), *Will teach for food: Academic labor in crisis* (pp. 279–290). Minneapolis: University of Minnesota Press.

Thompson, K. (2001). Faculty at the crossroads: Making the part-time problem a full-time focus. In E., Schell, and P. Stock (Eds.), *Moving a mountain: Transforming the role of non-tenure-track faculty in composition studies and higher education*. Urbana, IL: National Council of Teachers in English.

Thompson, K. (2003). Non-tenure track faculty and student learning: Welcome to the strativersity. *New Directions for Higher Education, 123*, 41–47.

Tirelli, V. (1997). Adjuncts and more adjuncts: Labor segmentations and the transformation of higher education. *Social Text, 51*, 75–91.

Tilly, C. (1996). *Half a job: Bad and good part-time jobs in a changing labor market*. Philadelphia: Temple University Press.

Tolbert, P. S. (1998). Two-tiered faculty systems and organizational outcomes. *New Directions for Higher Education, 104*, 71–80.

Toutkoushian, R. K., and Bellas, M. L. (2003). The effects of part-time employment and gender on faculty earnings and satisfaction: Evidence from the NSOPF–93. *Journal of Higher Education, 74*(2), 172–195.

Townsend, R. B. (2003). Changing relationships, changing values in the American classroom. *New Directions in Higher Education, 123*, 23–32.

Umbach, P. D. (2007). How effective are they? Exploring the impact of non-tenure track faculty on undergraduate education. *Review of Higher Education, 30*(2), 91–123.

Umbach, P. D. (2008, November). The effects of part-time faculty appointments on instructional techniques and commitment to teaching. Paper presented at the 33rd Annual Conference of the Association for the Study of Higher Education, Jacksonville, FL.

Wisneski, R. (2005). Investigating the research practices and library needs of non-tenure-track, tenure-track, and tenured English faculty. *Journal of Academic Librarianship, 31*(2), 119–133.

Worthen, H., and Berry, J. (2002). Bargaining for "quality" in higher education: A case study from the city colleges of Chicago. *Labor Studies Journal, 27*(3), 1–23.

Youn, T.I.K. (1988). Studies of academic markets and careers: An historical review. In D. W. Breneman and T.I.K. Youn (Eds.), *Academic labor markets and careers* (pp. 8–27). New York: Falmer.

Zahariadis, N. (2007). The multiple streams framework: Structure, limitations, prospects. In P. Sabatier (Ed.), *Theories of the policy process*. Boulder, CO: Westview Press.

Name Index

A

Alinsky, S., 36
Amacher, R. C., 43, 44
Anderson, E. L., 14
Anson, C. M., 19
Austin, A., 26, 43, 55, 61

B

Baldwin, R. G., 1, 2, 17, 23, 26, 34, 42, 45, 47, 52, 61
Banachowski, G., 11
Bataille, G. M., 55, 61
Bellas, M. L., 9, 22
Benjamin, E., 3, 31, 43, 44, 52, 54, 55, 58, 60, 61
Berry, J., 10, 36, 41, 51, 53
Bettinger, E., 31, 58
Bland, C., 9, 11, 29, 35, 53, 56, 58
Blau, G., 29
Bowen, H. R., 12
Boyer, E., 12
Bradburn, E. M., 3
Brand, M., 45
Bretz, R. D., Jr., 30
Brown, B. E., 55, 61
Burgan, M., 7, 43, 44
Burke, M., 36

C

Caplan, R. D., 30
Chait, R., 1, 9, 43, 44, 45
Chronister, J. L., 1, 2, 17, 23, 26, 34, 42, 45, 47, 52, 61

Connelly, C. E., 21
Cross, J. G., 1, 9, 10, 22, 23, 41, 42, 52
Curtis, J. W., 3

D

Darling-Hammond, L., 53
Davis, J., 59
DeCew, J. W., 51
Digranes, J.L.A., 57
Digranes, S. H., 57
Dobbie, D., 48, 51
Doeringer, P. B., 21
Dyer-Witheford, N., 16

E

Eagan, M. K., 11, 31, 58, 59, 60
Ehrenberg, R. G., 9, 16, 59, 60

F

Fahimi, M., 3
Farr, W. D., 27
Finkelstein, M. J., 1, 2, 3, 16, 23, 26, 55, 66
Finkin, M. W., 43
Ford, A. T., 1, 9
Forrest Cataldi, F. E., 3
Freeland, R. M., 56, 57

G

Gaff, J., 25, 26
Gallagher, D. G., 21
Gappa, J., 1, 2, 9, 12, 17, 26, 34, 42, 43, 45, 47, 48, 49, 52, 53, 55, 61

Toutkoushian, R. K., 9, 22
Townsend, R. B., 47
Trice, A., 26, 43, 52, 55, 61
Trower, C., 43, 44, 45, 1997

U

Umbach, P. D., 3, 9, 11, 21, 31, 32, 55,
  57, 60

W

Waller, R., 59

Weible, C. M., 70
Wisneski, R., 67
Worthen, H., 53

Y

Youn, T.I.K., 21

Z

Zahariadis, N., 70
Zhang, L., 9, 16, 59, 60

Subject Index

A

Accidental development versus conscious creation, 40–43
ACE (American Council on Education), 14, 15
Activism, 37
Adjunct Advocate, 14
Adjunct faculty, 5
Adjunct Nation, 14
Agency, 33
American Association for Higher Education (AAHE), 12
American Association of University Professors (AAUP), 43, 48, 49
American Council on Education (ACE), 14, 15
The American Faculty (Schuster and Finkelstein), 1
American Federation of Teachers (AFT), 5, 13–14, 48, 50
American Federation of Teachers Higher Education, 13
Association of American Universities (AAU), 14, 15
Assumptions of theoretical models, 37–38
Atheoretical research, 9

B

Bargaining units, 46, 47–48
Best practices: AFT's, 50
Boise State Institution, 54
Budget reforms, 42

C

California, 46
Call to action, 36–37
Commitment studies, 29
Commitment to teaching, 55–58
Community college students, 58–59
Composition changes in faculty, 1–2
Conscious creation versus accidental development, 40–43
Contact hours (faculty), 55–58
Context-based research, 67–68
Contextual analysis, 11
Contingent Academic Workers (CAW), 49–50
Contingent Appointments and the Academic Profession (AAUP), 48
Contingent faculty, 5, 73

D

Data. *See* studies/research
Deficit models, 28–29
Degree requirements, 54–55
Demographic shifts in faculty composition, 1–2
Departmental type, 68–69
Deprofessionalization/deskilling of faculty, 9, 27
Discipline/institutional type, 6, 9, 13, 68–69
Division of faculty groups, 46–47
Dual-market theory, 20–21

E

Economic theories, 9, 20–24, 71
Empirical research considerations, 59–62
Empirical tensions in research, 52–61
Employment conditions, 27–28
Environment: current faculty, 41
Evaluation: student, 54
Exploitation of non-tenure-track faculty, 8

F

Faculty: of color, 12; contact hours, 55–58;
  deprofessionalization/deskilling of, 9;
  divisions/tensions among, 45–47 (See also
  tensions); with doctorates, 21; FACE's
  recommendations for changes in, 50; full-
  time (See full-time non-tenure-track
  faculty); lenses for understanding, 33;
  motivations of, 22; non-tenure-track (See
  non-tenure-track positions); part-time
  (See part-time non-tenure-track faculty);
  quality of, 52, 53–54; responsibilities of,
  7; shifts in composition of, 1; subgroups,
  46; teaching styles, 57–58; temporary
  hires, 42; tenure-track (See tenured/
  tenure-track positions); terminology
  for tenure- and non-tenure-track, 4–5;
  women, 12, 22
Faculty and College Excellent (FACE)
  campaign, 50
Faculty Forum on Roles and Rewards of the
  American Association for Higher
  Education, 12
Full-time non-tenure-track faculty, 4–5, 38,
  65–66; AFT view of, 50; part-time
  versus, 46–47
Functionalist organizational theories, 34

G

Grade distribution and evaluation, 54
Grading patterns of full-time and part-time
  faculty, 54
Graduate assistants, 55
Graduate students, 22–23, 42
Graduation rates, 58–59
Groups studying non-tenure-track faculty,
  11–15

H

Heterogeneity, 10–11, 64–65
Higher Education Research Institute
  (HERI), 10
Higher education scholars, 12
Historical analysis, 11
Hybrid tenure structure, 44–45

I

Ideological tensions, 40–45
Ideology, 7–11
Indiana University case study, 45
Inequitable treatment, 14
Institutional theory, 36
Institutional type/discipline, 6, 9, 13,
  68–69
Instructional styles, 57–58
Interdisciplinary perspectives/studies, 9, 71

J

Job security, 21

L

Labor economists, 20–21
Labor laws, 46
Labor market principles, 22
Labor relations studies, 9
Labor relations theory, 35–37
Learning, 33
Liberal arts disciplines, 13
Literature review. See also studies/research:
  conflicting research, 7–11; deficits and
  assets, 38; differences in groups of non-
  tenure-track faculty, 13; lack of clarity in
  studies, 6; overview of, 1–3; terminology
  used, 4–7, 10, 73

M

Marching Towards Equity (AFT), 50
Maslow's theory of human motivation,
  32–33
Motivations of faculty, 22, 29–30, 68;
  Maslow's theory of human motivation,
  32–33
Multidisciplinary studies, 71

N

Narrow deficit conceptualization, 63–64
National Center for Education Statistics (NCES), 10, 54
National data, 66–67
National Education Association (NEA), 5, 13–14, 48, 49
National Education Association and The Contingent Academic Workers, 50
National Study of Post-secondary Faculty (NSOPF), 10
NCES (National Center for Education Statistics), 10, 54
NEA (National Education Association), 5, 13–14, 48
New Faculty Majority, 14
New Pathways Project, 12
New York, 46
Nondeficit-based studies, 69
Non-tenure-track positions, 22–23; addressing tensions of, 65–66; as challenge or solution to tenure, 43–45; compared to tenure-track, 43–44; conclusions about, 59–62; definitions/terminology used for, 4–7, 10, 73; determination of roles for, 39–40; development of research and policy, 72; as future model, 43–44; incentives for/influences on hiring, 41; needs/lives of, 67; relationships of, 70–71; rise in numbers of positions for, 12–13; start of proliferation of, 40–41; stereotypes of, 64; subgroups of, 11; theoretical examination of, 21
NSOPF (National Study of Post-secondary Faculty), 10

O

Organizational theory, 9, 34–35
Outcomes, student, 31–32

P

Part-time non-tenure-track faculty, 4–5, 22, 38, 65–66; AFT view of, 50; full time versus, 46–47; grade distribution of, 54
Policies/practices: change in tenure track,

3–4; development of, 72; focus of, 11; regarding faculty, 41; unions/ professional groups influencing, 48
Political economy theories, 9
Practical tensions, 45–51
Primary labor markets, 20–21
Priorities: of undergraduate education, 11
Productivity, 35, 57–58
Professionalization theory, 24–28
Psychological theory, 28–34

Q

Quality faculty, 53–54

R

Relationships: worker/organization, 21
Research. *See* studies/research
Resiliency theories, 69
Retention rates, 58–59

S

Secondary labor markets, 20–21
Senior Appointments with Reduced Loads (AAUP), 48
Social capital, 31
Social exchange theory, 21
Social psychological theory, 28–34
Sociological theories, 9
Sociological theory, 24–28
Southern Illinois University, 46
Standards of Good Practice in the Employment of Full-Time Non-Tenure-Track Faculty, 13
State data, 66–67
Stereotypes of non-tenure track faculty, 64
Student assistants, 55
Students: grade distribution and evaluation, 54; outcomes, 31–32; retention, transfer, and graduation rates, 58–59
Studies/research. *See also* literature review; theories/thoretical perspectives: changes in community colleges, 12; commitment of faculty, 29, 55–57; community college students, 58–59; context-based, 67–68; empirical tensions in, 52–62; experience/ understanding of non-tenure-track

faculty, 23; focus of, 20; groups studying non-tenure-track faculty, 11–15; heterogeneous nature of non-tenure-track faculty, 10–11; Indiana University case study, 45; interdisciplinary/multidisciplinary, 71; lack of meaningful data, 9–10; mixed/inconclusive results of, 69–70; National Study of Post-secondary Faculty (NSOPF), 10; nondeficit-based, 69; on non-tenure-track faculty, 13; recommendations for future, 51, 62, 66–71; research analysis, 4; strengthening of designs for, 65; understanding conflicts in, 7–11; undertheorized, 37; by unions, 13–14; vested interests of groups doing, 14–15

T

Teaching assistants, 11
Temporary hires, 42
Tensions: addressing, 65–66; empirical, 52–61; ideological, 40–45; practical, 45–51
Tenured/tenure-track positions: addressing tensions of, 65–66; compared to non-tenure track, 43–44; conclusions about, 59–62; costs of, 42; definitions/terminology, 4–7, 10, 73; needs/lives of, 67; perceived status quo of, 3; reforms for, 65
Tenure system, 35, 43–45, 48
Terminology, 4–7, 10, 73
Theories/theoretical perspectives. *See also* studies/research: application of, 19; assumptions of theoretical models,

37–38; atheoretical research, 9; critiques of, 20; dual-market theory, 20–21; economic theories, 9, 20–24, 71; functionalist organizational theories, 34; institutional theory, 36; labor relations theory, 35–37; Maslow's theory of human motivation, 32–33; missing perspectives in, 70–71; of non-tenure-track positions, 21; organizational theory, 9, 34–35; political economy theories, 9; professionalization theory, 24–28; resiliency theories, 69; social exchange theory, 21; social psychological theory, 28–34; sociological theories, 9; undertheorized studies, 37
"Theories Used to Study and Understand Non-Tenure-Track Faculty," 9
Transfer rates, 58–59
Trends: distinctions among, 5–6; historical, 11

U

Underemployment, 30
Undertheorized studies, 37
Unions, 8, 13–14, 36, 42, 47–51

V

The Vanishing Professor (AFT), 50
Vermont, 46

W

Women: preferences of employment of, 22; tenure-track positions for, 12